SUREŚVARA'S VĀRTIKA ON AŚVA AND AŚVAMEDHA BRĀHMAṆA

Sureśvara's Vārtika on Aśva and Aśvamedha Brāhmaṇa

Translated by
SHOUN HINO
K.P. JOG

MOTILAL BANARSIDASS PUBLISHERS
PRIVATE LIMITED • DELHI

First Edition: *Delhi, 1990*

ISBN: 81-208-0643-3

Also available at:

MOTILAL BANARSIDASS
41 U.A., Bungalow Road, Jawahar Nagar, Delhi 110 007
120 Royapettah High Road, Mylapore, Madras 600 004
24 Race Course Road, Bangalore 560 001
Ashok Rajpath, Patna 800 004
Chowk, Varanasi 221 001

PRINTED IN INDIA
BY JAINENDRA PRAKASH JAIN AT SHRI JAINENDRA PRESS, A-45 NARAINA INDUSTRIAL AREA, PHASE I, NEW DELHI 110 028 AND PUBLISHED BY NARENDRA PRAKASH JAIN FOR MOTILAL BANARSIDASS PUBLISHERS PVT. LTD., BUNGALOW ROAD, JAWAHAR NAGAR, DELHI 110 007.

To

Late Prof.
HIDENORI KITAGAWA
of
Nagoya University
(Japan)

PREFACE

The thought of undertaking a translation of the entire *Bṛhadāraṇyakopaniṣdbhāṣyavārtika* (Vārtika) of Sureśvara arose in our mind when Dr. Hino completed his translation of the Dialogue of Yājñavalkya and Maitreyī [(first) in the form of his Ph.D. Dissertation] which occurs in the *Bṛhadāraṇyakopaniṣad* in 2.4 and 4.5. Consequently, we began our translation of the Vārtika 2.5 called *Madhubrāhmaṇa* since it has an inseparable connection with the topic of Dr. Hino's work, as its complement. We thus happened to begin with the ending portions of the Madhukāṇḍa* which forms first two chapters of the *Bṛhadāraṇyakopaniṣad.* Now we turn to its beginning, viz. Vārtika 1.1 and 2 called respectively *Aśvabrāhmaṇa* and *Aśvamedhabrāhmaṇa.* These two form a bridge as it were between the ritualistic (*karmakāṇḍa*) and philosophical (*jñānakāṇḍa*) portions of the *Śatapathabrāhmaṇa.* Also, succeeding the *Sambandhavārtika* which fully develops the brief introductory of Śaṅkara to his Bhāṣya on the *Bṛhadāraṇyakopaniṣad* and is more or less an independent work of Sureśvara, it brings out in great detail Śaṅkara's thought in his Bhāṣya on the Upaniṣadic text proper.

Of course, it is needless to state, we follow the same method of translation etc. as in Dr. Hino's *Dialogue of Yājñavalkya and Maitreyī* in the Vārtika and our *Madhubrāhmaṇa* which is already published in 1988.

Seki-Gifu (*Japan*)
15*th March* 1989

Shoun Hino
K.P. Jog

*Cf. *Bṛhadāraṇyakavārtikasāra* of Vidyāraṇya 1.1.3: *bṛhadāraṇyake kāṇḍatrayam ādyam madhu smṛtam.*

TABLE OF CONTENTS

ABBREVIATIONS

AnSS	Ānandāśrama Sanskrit Series
BS	*Brahmasūtra*
BSB	*Brahmasūtrabhāṣya* by Śaṅkara
BU	*Bṛhadāraṇyakopaniṣad*
BUB	*Bṛhadāraṇyakopaniṣadbhāṣya* by Śaṅkara
BUBV	*Bṛhadāraṇyakopaniṣadbhāṣyavārtika* by Sureśvara
BVS	*Bṛhadāraṇyakavārtikasāra* by Vidyāraṇya
NKL	*Nyāyakalpalatikā*
SP	*Śāstraprakāśikā*

INTRODUCTION

Though the first two Brāhmaṇas in the Vārtika are called *Aśvabrāhmaṇa* and *Aśvamedhabrāhmaṇa*, we could call them both by one single name *Aśvamedhabrāhmaṇa* inasmuch as the two of them together have but one aim, viz. explaining the general purport of Śaṅkara's Bhāṣya which is revealed from a rather longish quotation from the same :

सर्वथाप्यस्त्यात्मा देहान्तरसंबन्धीत्येवं प्रतिपत्तुर्देहान्तरगतेष्टानिष्टप्राप्तिपरिहारोपायविशेषार्थिनस्तद्विशेषज्ञापनाय कर्मकाण्डमारब्धम् । न त्वात्मन इष्टानिष्टप्राप्तिपरिहारेच्छाकारणमात्मविषयमज्ञानं कर्तृभोक्तृस्वरूपाभिमानलक्षणं तद्विपरीतब्रह्मात्मस्वरूपविज्ञानेनापनीतम् । यावद्धि तन्नापनीयते तावदयं कर्मफलरागद्वेषादिस्वाभाविकदोषप्रयुक्तः शास्त्रविहितप्रतिषिद्धातिक्रमेणापि प्रवर्तमानो मनोवाक्कायैर्दृष्टादृष्टानिष्टसाधनान्यधर्मसंज्ञकानि कर्माण्युपचिनोति बाहुल्येन स्वाभाविकदोषबलीयस्त्वात् । ततः स्थावरान्ताधोगतिः ।

कदाचिच्छास्त्रकृतसंस्कारबलीयस्त्वम् । ततो मनआदिभिरिष्टसाधनं बाहुल्येनोपचिनोति धर्माख्यम् । तद्द्विविधम्—ज्ञानपूर्वकं केवलं च । तत्र केवलं पितृलोकादिप्राप्तिफलम् । ज्ञानपूर्वकं देवलोकादिब्रह्मलोकान्तप्राप्तिफलम् । तथा च शास्त्रम् 'आत्मयाजी श्रेयान्देवयाजिनः' इत्यादि । स्मृतिश्च 'द्विविधं कर्म वैदिकम्' इत्याद्या । साम्ये च धर्माधर्मयोर्मनुष्यत्वप्राप्तिः । एवं ब्रह्माद्या स्थावरान्ता स्वाभाविकाविद्यादिदोषवतो धर्माधर्मसाधनकृता संसारगतिर्नामरूपकर्माश्रया ।

तदेवेदं व्याकृतं साध्यसाधनरूपं जगत् प्रागुत्पत्तेरव्याकृतमासीत् । स एष बीजाङ्कुरादिवदविद्याकृतः संसार आत्मनि क्रियाकारकफलाध्यारोपलक्षणोऽनादिरनन्तोऽनर्थ इत्येतस्माद्विरक्तस्याविद्यानिवृत्तये तद्विपरीतब्रह्मविद्याप्रतिपत्त्यर्थोपनिषदारभ्यते ।

अस्य त्वश्वमेधकर्मसंबन्धिनो विज्ञानस्य प्रयोजनम् । येषामश्वमेधे नाधिकारस्तेषामस्मादेव विज्ञानात्तत्फलप्राप्तिः 'विद्यया वा कर्मणा वा', 'तद्धैतल्लोकजिदेव' इत्येवमादिश्रुतिभ्यः ।

कर्मविषयत्वमेव विज्ञानस्येति चेत् । न । 'योऽश्वमेधेन यजते य उ चैनमेवं वेद' इति विकल्पश्रुतेः । विद्याप्रकरणे चाम्नानात् । कर्मान्तरे च संपादनदर्शनाद्विज्ञानात्तत्फलप्राप्तिरस्तीत्यवगम्यते । सर्वेषां च कर्मणां परं कर्माश्वमेधः । समष्टिव्यष्टिप्राप्तिफलत्वात् ।

तस्य चेह ब्रह्मविद्याप्रारम्भ आम्नानं सर्वकर्मणां संसारविषयत्वप्रदर्शनार्थम् । तथा च दर्शयिष्यति फलमशनाया मृत्युभावम् ।

न नित्यानां संसारविषयफलत्वमिति चेत् । न । सर्वकर्मफलोपसंहारश्रुतेः । सर्वं हि पत्नीसंबद्धं कर्म कर्म 'जाया मे स्यादेतावान्वै कामः' इति निसर्गत एव सर्वकर्मणां काम्यत्वं दर्शयित्वा, पुत्रकर्मापरविद्यानां च 'अयं लोकः पितृलोको देवलोकः' इति फलं दर्शयित्वा त्र्यन्नात्मकतां चान्त उपसंहरिष्यति 'त्रयं व इदं नाम रूपं कर्म' इति । सर्वकर्मणां फलं व्याकृतं संसार एवेति ।

इदमेव त्रयं प्रागुत्पत्तेस्तर्ह्यव्याकृतमासीत् । तदेव पुनः सर्वप्राणिकर्मवशाद्व्याक्रियते बीजादिव वृक्षः । सोऽयं व्याकृताव्याकृतरूपः संसारोऽविद्याविषयः क्रियाकारकफलात्मकतयात्मरूपत्वेनाध्यारोपितोऽविद्ययैव मूर्तामूर्ततद्वासनात्मकः । अतो विलक्षणोऽनामरूपकर्मात्मकोऽद्वयो नित्यशुद्धबुद्धमुक्तस्वभावोऽपि क्रियाकारकफलभेदादिविपर्ययेणावभासते । अतोऽस्मात्क्रियाकारकफलभेदस्वरूपादेतावदिदमिति साध्यसाधनरूपाद्विरक्तस्य कामादिदोषकर्मबीजभूताविद्यानिवृत्तये रज्ज्वामिव सर्पविज्ञानापनयाय ब्रह्मविद्यारभ्यते ॥

It is not necessary for our purpose to translate the whole of this passage here, yet the substance of Śaṅkara's argument is: Generally one performs the rituals prescribed in the scriptural texts; these performances by one are marked by desires. While performing these, one does not consider the teachings of the Upaniṣads, the concluding portion of the scriptures and, therefore, attains worldly prosperity and subsequently, after death, a happy abode in the heaven. As against this, if one has understood the teachings of the Upaniṣads, one's *citta* is purified and then the way for the knowledge of the non-dual Brahman is opened for one and this knowledge secures for one liberation.

Now we should pay particular attention to the lines:

अस्य त्वश्वमेधकर्मसंबन्धिनो विज्ञानस्य प्रयोजनम् । येषामश्वमेधे नाधिकारस्तेषामस्मादेव विज्ञानात्तत्फलप्राप्तिः । 'विद्यया वा कर्मणा वा', 'तद्धैतल्लोकजिदेव' इत्येवमादिश्रुतिभ्यः । कर्मविषयत्वमेव विज्ञानस्येति चेत् ।

न 'योऽश्वमेधेन यजते य उ चैनमेवं वेद' इति विकल्पश्रुतेः। विद्याप्रकरणे चाम्नानात्। कर्मान्तरे च संपादनदर्शनाद्विज्ञानात्तत्फलप्राप्तिरस्तीत्यवगम्यते। सर्वेषां च कर्मणां परं कर्माश्वमेधः। समष्टिव्यष्टिप्राप्तिफलत्वात्। तस्य चेह ब्रह्मविद्याप्रारम्भ आम्नानं सर्वकर्मणां संसारविषयत्वप्रदर्शनार्थम्। तथा च दर्शयिष्यति फलमशनाया मृत्युभावम्।

Śaṅkara points to the significance of the knowledge of the Real (i.e. Brahman), viz. it directly secures liberation as an alternative for performance of ritual which, as stated above, leads only to the purification of *citta* that is a step towards liberation. Even the knowledge of the Aśvamedha, viz. the awareness of the nature of the ritual and its result as some (i.e. gross or subtle—the former more) manifestation of the Real (i.e. Brahman) and *not necessarily the performance* of the ritual is a means to liberation. This view of Śaṅkara finds support in the Śrutis: *Śatapathabrāhmaṇa* 10.4.3.9; BU 1.3.28 and *Taittirīya Saṁhitā* 5.3.12.2.

This is, in fact, the purport of the first two Brāhmaṇas. Yet the two Brāhmaṇas refer respectively to (i) the *dravya* etc.[1] and (ii) the *devatā* viz. Agni.

They refer to the Upāsanā 'worship' of the Brahman in its manifest form. Thus,

(i) the first Brāhmaṇa refers to the Upāsanā of the horse and its limbs to be molested in the sacrifice, and the two *grahas* contained in golden and silver cups, called Mahimā-*grahas*;

(ii) the second Brāhmaṇa refers to the Upāsanā of Agni.

It is then maintained that these two Upāsanās, which are really but one Upāsanā as discussed in BUBV 1.2.211-218, result into the Upāsaka's becoming one with Hiraṇyagarbha or Sūtrātman, the prime sacrificer, and finally being liberated from every body as stated in BUBV 1.2.219-227.

Yet, before coming to the conclusion of 1.2, the seer of the Upaniṣad has found it necessary to discuss how the common performer of an Aśvamedha sacrifice **dies** and then becomes, owing to the merit (*apūrva* or *dharma*), one with the prime sacrificer, who is a manifest (though minutest) form of the Brahman owing to overpowering Māyā 'Ignorance about the ultimate reality', how this **death** is different from the common death, and how subsequently even this prime sacrificer, who will have overcome this Ignorance, becomes one with the Brahman. All this discussion necessarily implies the Satkāraṇavāda (of Śaṅkara's system of philosophy) and therefore affords Sureśvara an occasion to discuss the *kāraṇa-kārya* relation between the ultimate reality and the human body which through sacrifice becomes one with that of the prime sacrificer and finally secures ultimate release from bondage, or, in other words, the resultant oneness with the formless Brahman. Again, in the course of this discussion, Sureśvara has found it necessary to discuss some views, particularly the views regarding cause and effect relation, of the logicians and followers of some of the Buddhist schools. Further, it has become necessary for him to explain how the prime sacrificer, Prajāpati, is known by other names, Agni, Arka, Aditi and Mṛtyu—in fact, this is the principal topic of discussion in BU, BUB and BUBV.

It is obvious from the preceding that BU and, therefore, BUBV (1.1 and 1.2) do not involve into any detailed examination of various philosophical positions. They only make certain assertions whose examination in every detail follows in later sections of the two works.

Here, a few words are necessary in connection with Sureśvara's work on BUB which is called Vārtika 'an examination of what is said, unsaid or wrongly said (in the work, viz. Bhāṣya, under comment)'[2]. In other words, a Vārtika fully develops even the implied thoughts in the work (and also occasionally modifies them). In BUBV 1.2.57-64 Sureśvara has felt the need for bringing out the full import of Śaṅkara's comment *sādṛśyād anvayadarśanaṁ na kāraṇānuvṛtter iti cen na* (BUB p. 21). Here 'Śaṅkara has omitted to give the argument of the opponent which is based on the supposition that the relation of cause and effect can only be apprehended by comparison.'[3] In connection with this, Ānandagiri's comment on BUB finds a basis in Sureśvara's explanation in the BUBV. Again, Sureśvara offers in BUBV 1.2.149 an etymological explanation of the name Arka, though BUB does not say anything in respect of the same. Also noteworthy is Sureśvara's comment on *katham abhivyaktiliṅgatvād abhivyaktiliṅgam asyeti* ... (BUB p. 22) in BUBV 1.2.81-87. These are examples of examination of what is unsaid (*anukta*) in the Bhāṣya; here he clarifies the implication in the comment by Śaṅkara.

Yet more interesting is BUBV 1.2.170-171 which expresses Sureśvara's own view regarding the connection between BU 1.2.1-3 and 1.2.4. This is entirely beside the view of Śaṅkara and can be called as Sureśvara's *udbhāṣya* writing.

Attention can be invited to BUBV 1.2.146 wherein Sureśvara controverts Śaṅkara's comment on *āpo 'jāyanta* (BUB pp. 29-30 on BU 1.2.1) and offers his own explanation. This can be considered as *duruktacintā*.

Incidentally, a case may be pointed out where Sureśvara shows some difference of opinion with Śaṅkara; that is his interpretation of *sa tayā vācā* (BU 1.2.5). It reveals his independent outlook.

This brief notice of a fairly small portion of BUBV should raise a scholar's hope to find in the remaining part of the work more data for determining the value of Sureśvara's contribution to Śaṅkara's school of Vedānta.

While concluding this brief introduction, it is only imperative first to make some general observation regarding BU 1.1-2. These two Brāhmaṇas reveal that the Brahmanical tendency to assert the identity of what might be called as two (almost entirely) unconnected things—this is described as expression of Bandhutā Philosophy—paves way to the convenient means of the Vedānta for abstracting one's mind from the worldly life, concentrating for some time on some non-Brahman thing, and then later on the Brahman itself. Upāsanās prescribed in BU 1.1-2 thus mark the source of the gradual steps for a seeker of the Brahman. The Prajāpati or Hirṇyagarbha is identified in BU 1.1-2 as Aśva, Arka, Samudra, Aditi, Mṛtyu, Āditya; all these displaying the various manifestations (*nāmarūpābhyāṁ vyākaraṇa*) of the Brahman. Mṛtyu however is the most important of them, for Mṛtyu in ordinary life is death, the cessation of an active worldly body. However, here in the BU, Mṛtyu is the first and the minutest manifestation of the Brahman—a sacrificer with all pure thoughts, free from almost all influence of Māyā, and nearmost to the state of the Brahman. This is why the BU which succeeds the ritual portion of the *Śatapathabrāhmaṇa* has time and again stressed on the need for a human being to endeavour to become one with Mṛtyu (*mṛtyvātmabhāva*); of course, only by way of concession to those who look upon rituals as ancillary to attaining the knowledge of the Brahman. Mṛtyu is thus in this context cessation of the cycle or chain of worldly life.

And, now, we should express deep sense of indebtedness to the commentaries *Śāstraprakāśikā* and *Nyāyakalpalatikā*, without the help of which there could have resulted on our part only frustration with regard to the knotty problems which Sureśvara's Vārtikas present time and again.

Notes:

[1]*kāla*, *loka* and other elements connected with the Aśvamedha sacrifice.

[2]Cf. Rājaśekhara's definition: *uktānuktaduruktacintā vārttikam*/ *Kāvyamimāṁsā*, p. 5, lines 7-8 (Gaekwad's Oriental Series No. 1, Baroda: 1934).

[3]Cf. *The Twelve Principal Upaniṣads*, p. 21 (E. Röer, vol. 2, Madras: 1931).

BṚHADĀRAṆYAKOPANIṢAD-BHĀṢYA-VĀRTIKA

(BUBV 1.1)

Aśvabrāhmaṇa

तत्राश्वविषयं तावदादौ दर्शनमुच्यते ॥
प्राजापत्यत्वहेतोश्चाप्यश्वनामाङ्कितत्वतः ॥ १ ॥

To begin with, there is in the beginning of the Upaniṣad discussed (lit. mentioned) the worship (lit. seeing[1]) which has the horse as its object, because it is the means, firstly, for being the means to obtain the nature (or the status) of Prajāpati[2] and, secondly, because it is marked by the name 'a horse'. [1]

[1]This refers to the Upāsanā connected with a horse, viz. the Aśvamedha sacrifice, and consequently with Fire in its various forms which are mentioned in the last portions of BUBV 1.2. Cf. also BUBV 1.2.1; 220.

[2]This is a reference to the first manifest form, the most minute one, of the Brahman, viz. Hiraṇyagarbha, which is discussed in BUBV 1.2 at length.

अश्वस्य यच्छिरः साक्षात्तदुषा इति चिन्तयेत् ॥
हरेरवयवेष्वेवं योज्याः कालादिदृष्टयः ॥ २ ॥

[This gives the meaning of the Upaniṣadic sentence *uṣā vā aśvasya śiraḥ* (BU 1.2.1). The second line explains the BU sentence *sūryaś cakṣur...*]

One should think (i.e. meditate on) that what is (i.e. knows as) the head of a horse[1] is the directly perceptible Uṣas. (Thus) should one[2] entertain (further) the notions of *kāla* etc.[3] in respect of the (different) limbs of the horse (of the sacrifice). [2]

[1]The horse refers to the horse of the Aśvamedha sacrifice.

[2]It is known in the Upaniṣad that while getting to know the Brahman one has first to understand some manifest object as the Brahman and later does one gradually come to realize the nature of the nameless, formless, qualityless Brahman. Therefore, there is in the beginning mention made of the worship of some object, e.g. Aśvamedha etc., which is to be connected with the knowledge of the Brahman (*jñānakarmasamuccaya*). Cf. BUBV 1.3.1-3; BS 4.1.6. Read: *utkṛṣṭadṛṣṭir hīne syāt*—BVS p. 181, verse 19. Also BSB 4.1.5: *brahmadṛṣṭir evādityādiṣu syāt—kasmāt/utkarṣāt/evam utkarṣeṇādityādayo dṛṣṭā bhavanti.*

[3]The word 'etc.' refers to other aspects connected with the Aśvamedha sacrifice.

संस्कार्यत्वात्पशोरेवं दृष्टीरङ्गेषु योजयेत् ॥
कालादावमखाङ्गत्वान्नाश्वदृष्टिर्विधित्स्यते ॥ ३ ॥

Since the animal (viz. horse) is to be sanctified (for the performance), one should entertain such notions (as *kāla* etc.) in respect of its (different) limbs. (However) since *kāla* etc. are not the parts of the sacrifice, therefore entertaining the notion of them as a horse (or its limbs) is not sought to be prescribed (by the Śruti).[1] [3]

[1]Such notion is set aside by BS 4.1.6: *ādityādimatayaś cāṅga upapatteḥ.*

सत्स्वश्वादिषु कालादिदृष्टीरङ्गेषु योजयेत् ॥
असत्स्वात्मानमेवाश्वं कल्पयित्वा नियोजयेत् ॥ ४ ॥

One should entertain the notions of *kāla* etc. in respect of the limbs of the horse (of the sacrifice) when the horse etc. are present (i.e. actually connected with the ritual[1]). But when there is no presence of a horse and its limbs[2] one should entertain (the notions) only after imagining one's own body[3] as that of a horse. [4]

[1]SP points out that this has a reference to the performance of the Aśvamedha by one who is entitled to undertake it.

[2]This is in respect of one who is not entitled to the performance of the sacrifice.

[3]The word *ātman* refers to the body (SP). Read BVS p. 181, verse 18:

upāsanasya svātantryāt karmānadhikṛto 'pi ca/
manasā kalpayitvāśvaṁ virāḍrūpeṇa cintayet//

कर्तारमश्वमग्निं च चित्यं सर्वं प्रजापतिम् ॥
अश्वमेधफलं चार्कं वेत्ति मृत्युं यथोदितम् ॥ ५ ॥

अकर्ताऽप्यश्वमेधस्य ब्राह्मणश्चेह बुद्धिमान् ॥
क्रत्वात्मा मृत्युरस्मीति तादात्म्यं सोऽधिगच्छति ॥ ६ ॥

And the wise Brāhmaṇa[1], even though a non-performer of the Aśvamedha, who knows about the performance of the sacrifice, the horse and the fire which is to be collected (from whatever house of (a fire worshiper)—all (this) as Prajāpati, Arka, the result of the (performance of the) Aśvamedha sacrifice), and Mṛtyu as stated (in the later portion of the text) secures oneness with him (Mṛtyu or the Sūtrātman)[2] on (knowing) 'I am the soul of the sacrifice, Mṛtyu'. [5-6]

[1]Brāhmaṇa indicates Kṣatriya and Vaiśya who also are eligible for the performance of the Aśvamedha.

[2]SP refers to the view that entertaining the various notions which are considered as the objects of different Upāsanās would bring in here a *vākyabheda* 'prescription of more things than one by only one sentence' and then it points out that since these (so called Upāsanās) have but one result and not various results, there is no *vākyabheda*; all these notions go to form but one Upāsanā.

अश्वसंज्ञपनात्पूर्वं तथोर्ध्वं चापि हाटक-
राजतात्मकपात्राभ्यां गृह्येते तत्र यौ ग्रहौ ॥
महिमाख्यौ तयोरेतदहर्वा इति दर्शनम् ॥ ७ ॥

The sentence in the Śruti (lit. in what is heard text) *ahar vā...* has a reference to the two cups (in the performance of the

Aśvamedha sacrifice containing the offering material), one made of gold and the other of silver, which are taken[1] before and after molesting the horse in the sacrifice, and called Mahiman. [7]

[1]Read SP: *graho havanīyadravyayuktapātraviśeṣaḥ|tayor graho mantrasaṁskṛtayor upādānam|* (*graho* is *grahaṇam* 'drinking (from it'))

व्यत्ययेनावबोद्धव्या प्रथमार्थे च सप्तमी ॥ ८ ॥
समुद्र ईश्वरो ज्ञेयो योनिः कारणमुच्यते ॥
सर्वस्य जगतो यस्मादीश एवेह कारणम् ॥ ९ ॥

(In the sentence *samudra eva*) the locative case is to be understood by interchange for the nominative [8]
(thus giving rise to the sense:) 'Let the sea[1] be known as the Lord.' The word *yoni* is used here for (conveying the sense:) the source or cause. (This is so) because the Lord himself is, for this Śāstra, the source of all (the universe). [9]

[1]SP gives the derivation of *samudra* thus: *samutpadya bhūtāni dravanty asminn iti*. Incidentally, after explaining the meaning of *yoni* 'source', SP adds: *bandhuśabdasyāpy ayam evārthaḥ| tatra* (i) *yonitvam utpādakatvam* (ii) *bandhutvaṁ sthāpakatvam* (iii) *samudrātā vilāpakatvam iti bhedaḥ|* He thus refers to *utpatti*, *sthiti* and *pralaya*. Cf. BS 1.1.2: *janmādy asya yataḥ|*

|| iti prathamādhyāyasya prathamam aśvabrāhmaṇaṁ samāptam||

BṚHADĀRAṆYAKOPANIṢAD-BHĀṢYA-VĀRTIKA

(BUBV 1.2)

Aśvamedha Brāhmaṇa

अथाग्नेरुच्यते जन्म हयमेधोपयोगिनः ॥
तद्दर्शनविधित्सार्थं स्तुत्यर्थोत्पत्तिरिष्यते ॥ १ ॥

Now is stated the origination of fire which is useful for (the performance etc. of) the Aśvamedha. (Then) with the intention to prescribe the worship (lit. seeing) of it, it is desired (to state) its origination for the sake of praise. [1]

After stating the Upāsanā 'worship' connected with the Aśvamedha and particularly the two Mahimāgrahas, the text now states about the worship of fire; cf. SP 1.1.1 and BUBV 1.2.220 below. The philosophical purpose is pointed out here. The words of the BU *naiveha*...do not have any reference to fire, yet it indicates the worship of fire. We do not take fire in the sense of the element. What is meant is the fire used for the performance of the Homa. Read SP: *agnidarśanasya vidhātum iṣṭasya vidhyartham agnistutiphalā tadutpattir iṣṭā/śuddhajanmatvād utkṛṣṭatvenāyam upāsyo rājādivad ity arthaḥ/*

नामवद्रूपवच्चेह कारणं यावदीक्ष्यते ॥
नाभूत्तत्प्राक्समुत्पत्तेः प्राणाद्युत्पत्तिसंश्रवात् ॥ २ ॥

(Verses 2-5 are an objector's view on the non-existence of both the cause and the effect. Verses 2 and 5 are the opinion of the Śūnyavādin and verses 3 and 4, of the Asatkāryavādin.)

Whatever is here accepted (lit. thought) as the cause has a name and a form. (But that) did not exist before its origination, (this we say) since there is a mention (in the Śruti) of the origin of Prāṇa etc.[1] [2]

Here the Śūnyavādin, who holds that there is total absence of any cause and its effect, argues that the Śruti says: 'Prāṇa was born', cf. verse 142 below. This means that it was not existent before for the reason that formerly the cause and the effect were not existent.

[1]SP: *prāṇaḥ sūkṣmaḥ prapañcaḥ/ādiśabdaḥ sthūlaprapañcārthaḥ/*

कार्यमुत्पत्तिमत्त्वाच्चेत्प्रागुत्पत्तेर्निषिध्यते ॥
कारणस्य त्वनुत्पत्तेरनिषेधस्तथा सति ॥ ३ ॥

[Verses 3 and 4 are views of the Asatkāryavādin and verse 5 makes an answer to these two by the Śūnyavādin.]

If, on account of its having origination, an effect is rejected (as existing) before its origination, then the cause could not be rejected just because it has not originated. [3]

A view of another Pūrvapakṣin, who is Asatkāryavādin—a follower of Kaṇāda—is stated in this verse. He holds that the cause and the effect both did not exist before the creation of the effect; only the cause existed; this points to the purposelessness of the Śruti statement: *naiveha*..; cf. SP: *siddhasādhyatvenāsatkāryavādi dūṣayati*. According to this Pūrvapakṣin, Agni's origination is acceptable, because it did not exist before. However, its cause did exist, since its origination has not been mentioned.

तथा चानुपलब्धेश्च कार्यस्यैवास्तु नास्तिता ॥
कारणस्य न नास्तित्वमुक्तहेत्वोरसंभवात् ॥ ४ ॥

So also, owing to the non-perception (of the effect), let there be (accepted) the non-existence of the effect alone. The absence of the cause however does not follow, because of the impossibility of these two reasons (in respect of it)[1]. [4]

[1]*Anupalabdhi* 'non-perception' is another Pramāṇa for acce-

pting the non-existence of fire before its origination. However, in respect of its cause, *Anupalabdhi* does not hold good; the Śruti clearly states its existence in *vāyor agniḥ* etc.

सर्वस्यानुपलब्धेस्तु मैवं वोचो यतः श्रुतिः ॥
नैवेह किंचनेत्याह कारणेतरनिह्नुतिम् ॥ ५ ॥

(The Śūnyavādin says:) 'But on account of the non-perception of all this (viz. both the cause and the effect), do not say so, since the Śruti passage *naiveha kiṁcana*...has declared the absence (lit. concealment) of (both) the cause and the other (viz. the effect). [5]

Though the followers of Kaṇāda said that only the effect did not exist before its origination and the cause did exist, the Śruti contradicts their view on the basis of the Śruti *naiveha kiṁcana*. This is the answer of the Śūnyavādin.

This concludes the statement of the view(s) of the Pūrvapakṣins.

नैवं यतः श्रुतिः साक्षात्सत्त्वमेवावदत्स्वयम् ॥
कार्यकारणयोः स्पष्टं मृत्युनैवेति सादरा ॥ ६ ॥

[Verses 6-10 are an answer to the views of the Pūrvapakṣins.]

(This is) not so, because the Śruti[1] itself which has (full) regard (for the following statement:) *mṛtyunaiva*..., has declared the existence of (both) the cause and the effect in clear terms. [6]

[1]The Śruti pertains to the object which is unmanifest and which has no name and form. Further that Śruti, which is controverted by the Pūrvapakṣins, and the subsequent Śruti, viz. *mṛtyunaiva*..., delcare the existence of both the cause and the effect. In the earlier part of the Śruti is stated the non-existence of the cause and the effect but in the later, the existence of both.

मृत्युना कारणेनेदं कार्यं सर्वं समावृतम् ॥
इति नावक्ष्यद्यद्येतदुभयं नाभवत्पुरा ॥ ७ ॥

If both of these (i.e. the cause and the effect) did not exist before, the Śruti would not have declared all this (that is called) effect as covered by the cause, viz. Mṛtyu.[1] [7]

[1]This verse explains BUB *yadi hi kiṁcid api nāsīd yenāvriyate yac cāvriyate tadā nāvakṣyan mṛtyunaivedam āvṛtam iti* / This points to the existence of both the cause and the effect even before the latter originated from the former. The next verse explains the significance of the word *mṛtyu.*

प्राणपिण्डादिकार्याणां समुद्रः परमेश्वरः ॥
बन्धुः कारणमात्मोक्तो मृत्युरत्र स एव तु ॥ ८ ॥

ज्ञानमात्रसतत्त्वं यद्ब्रह्माज्ञातसतत्त्वकम् ॥
मृत्युर्जनिमतः साक्षात्तत्र कार्याप्ययत्वतः ॥ ६ ॥

In the case of the effects such as Prāṇa, body[1] etc., the Supreme Lord (i.e. the maker) is Samudra. It is also (the great) relative, the cause, the Ātman—it is only He who is mentioned here by the term Mṛtyu. [8]

The Brahman, which is of the nature[2] of mere knowledge and whose nature is not known, is indeed but Mṛtyu in the case of whatever has birth, since there in that occurs the merger of all that is effect. [9]

Verses 8 and 9 explain the significance of the term Mṛtyu. It does not mean 'Death' as commonly understood. Reference is made here to *samudra evāsya bandhuḥ samudra evāsya yoniḥ* which is at the end of 1.1 above. The words *bandhu* and *kāraṇa* are synonymous.

[1]*prāṇa* and *piṇḍa* refer to the collective and the individual forms.

[2]The word *satattva* means *yāthātmya* (NKL).

सद्बीजं सत्प्रतिष्ठं च सदायतनमेव च ।
प्रत्यक्षमेव सत्सिद्धं सदन्यस्याप्रसिद्धितः ॥ १० ॥

Whatever existent obtains under our eyes (i.e. is directly perceptible) has an existent as its origin, an existent as its support and an existent as its abode,[1] because anything else than the existent[2] is not known. [10]

[1]The verse seeks to establish that all that is existent has originated in some existent. Thus it affirms its acceptance of Satkāryavāda.

[2]This is non-existent (*asat*) which could be imagined by one as the origin of what is directly perceptible existent.

असत्सदतिरेकेण यदि वाव्यतिरेकतः ॥
व्यतिरेके सदेवासदसद्वा तत्किमुच्यते ॥ ११ ॥

[Verses 11-16 explain why there does not obtain any non-existent which is the origin as hinted in verse 10 above.]

Here one would ask whether or not a non-existent stands apart from (i.e. is distinct from) an existent and?, in case it is distinct, is the non-existent itself not extant or what is (called) non-existent is extant[1]? [11]

[1]If a non-existent is considered to be distinct from an existent, then it must have some distinguishing property which does not allow it to remain a non-existent: cf. SP : *asad api sad eva syād bhedadharmitvād ghaṭavat* |

नेह सद्व्यतिरेकेण स्वमहिम्ना प्रसिध्यति ॥
सर्वस्य सदपेक्षत्वात्सत्तु नान्यदपेक्षते ॥ १२ ॥

Here (in this world) there does not obtain a non-existent apart from an existent on its own strength (lit. greatness), since all (that is existent) expects (i.e. depends upon) another existent[1] (as its origin, its support and its abode). But whatever is existent does not expect any other (origin, support or abode).[2] [12]

[1]This is said with the view that there is no possibility of

accepting any such discrete objects as existent and non-existent.

[2]This argument proceeds from the notion: An existent is different from a non-existent, which is different in nature. The answer refers to the existent, viz. the Brahman, which is self-luminous; it does not expect the denial (*apoha*) of any non-existent.

मतमव्यतिरेकेण सतोऽसत्सत्तदिष्यताम् ॥
कुतोऽदो लभतेऽसत्त्वं यत्सदात्मनि निष्ठितम् ॥ १३ ॥

If it is held that the non-existent does not exist apart from the existent, then let that be accepted as an existent. Why does it get the character of a non-existent, since (i.e. if) it is supported[1] in what has the nature of the existent. [13]

[1]This more or less means 'is identical with'.

अन्योन्यव्यतिरेकित्वान्नान्योन्यात्मकता तयोः ॥
विरोधित्वाच्च नान्योन्यं संबन्धस्तापशीतवत् ॥ १४ ॥

(Then) since they exist apart from each other, the two are not of the nature of each other and, since they are opposed to each other (in nature), they do not have any mutual relation as (there does not exist any) between heat and cold. [14]

In the previous verse, it was pointed out that the existent and the non-existent cannot be described as distinct from each other. Now it is stated that the two cannot be described as non-distinct either.

स्फुरताऽपि सतो नान्यदभिधातुं घटादिवत् ॥
शक्यते नाभिधानेन ह्यसद्वस्तु निरुच्यते ॥ १५ ॥

Even if there were to exist (according to someone[1]) some relation, it is not possible for anyone to mention any non-existent by name as (one would be able to mention) a pot. Indeed, a non-existent is never (or can never be) described by any name. [15]

This proceeds from the fact that use of words is possible only in the case of objects having some distinct characteristic or form. A non-existent cannot have it and therefore no words can be used to refer to any of its relation to the existent.

[1]Literally, *sphuratā* = *prājñena* 'some one very intelligent (who might see such a relation)'.

वस्तुनोऽतिशयः कश्चिदभाववचसोच्यते ॥
तस्य तेनाभिसंव्याप्तेर्न कथंचिदपह्नुतिः ॥ १६ ॥

An excellence of a thing is described by the statement of non-existence (of some defects etc.); since that (excellence) pervades that (thing), there cannot be concealment of the same (excellence) in any way. [16]

क्रिया वा तत्फलं वा स्यादभावो नात्महेतुहा ॥
यो यतो लभते सत्तां निरुणद्धि स तं कथम् ॥ १७ ॥

न नाशो हन्ति नष्टारं गन्तारमिव तद्गतिः ॥
यो यतो लिप्सते सिद्धिं स तं हन्ति कथं वद ॥ १८ ॥

[Verses 17-19 deny destruction of the cause of this (apparently) existent world. Verses 17-18 refer to Logicians who follow Kaṇāda and verse 19 refers to the Vijñānavādin (Yogācāra view) (NKL).]

Non-existence could be either an action or its result. But it would not destroy its own cause. (For) how can a thing which requires its existence from whatsoever (source), destroy (lit. stop) that? [17]

Destruction does not destroy the destroyer even as the going of one does not (destroy) the goer. (Just) tell me, how it can destroy that from which it wishes to obtain some acquisition (viz. existence.) [18]

Earlier the author set aside the existence of any non-existent beside the existent. And now he disputes even the destruction of some existent cause which could possibly be posited by someone. The verse intends to set aside the Logicians' notion that an existent pitcher—an effect—did not exist before and that it originated through *dhvaṁsa*. The author shows that *dhvaṁsa* can be either an action or a result and cannot therefore destroy its cause (*ātmahetuhā*). The second line hints at the presence of clay etc. even when the effect, viz. a pot, has come into existence.

विज्ञानाव्यतिरेकी चेदभावः स्यात्सहेतुकः ॥
ध्वंसादव्यतिरेकेऽपि धियो नित्यत्वमापतेत् ॥ १९ ॥

If destruction is not distinct from Idea (*vijñāna*), then how could it have a cause[1]? If (on the other hand) Idea were to be considered distinct from destruction, there would follow only eternity[2]. [19]

The whole argument is based on the view that *dhvaṁsa* (= *abhāva*) has an origin (*hetu*) and it is eternal. This sets aside a possible opposition by the Vijñānavādin, who would equate *dhvaṁsa* with Idea. There are two possibilities: (a) *dhvaṁsa* is non-distinct from Idea, and (b) Idea is not distinct from *dhvaṁsa* either.

(1) This is to answer away (a). *dhvaṁsa*, being (pre-) *dhvaṁsa* of something, has some origin (i.e. cause). Therefore, it cannot be like Idea, without any cause, and therefore momentary.

(2) An answer to (b). If Idea (*dhī*) were to be non-distinct from *dhvaṁsa*, it would be permanent like *dhvaṁsa*—an unacceptable proposition for the Vijñānavādins.

अतोऽभावत्वसिद्ध्यर्थमभावेनाप्यपेक्ष्यते ॥
स्वहेतुसिद्धिः कार्योऽर्थो न दृष्टः कारणं विना ॥ २० ॥

धर्म्यसिद्धिः प्रतिज्ञायां हेतुश्चानाश्रयो भवेत् ॥
न चास्ति कश्चिद्दृष्टान्तः सर्वशून्यत्ववादिनः ॥ २१ ॥

[The argument in these verses is against the Mādhyamika

view: *sarvaṁ śūnyam*—in other words: *sarvasya dhvaṁsasiddhiḥ.*]

Therefore[1] in order that there results non-existence, non-existence also[2] would expect the existence of its cause[3]; for, a thing, which is an effect, is not seen (to have come into existence) without a cause.[4] [20]
If one were to state the enunciation ('All this world was absolutely non-existent'), there is not established any (subject[5]) having any property; then the reason[6] would be without any basis and also there is not any example[7] for the Śūnyavādin who negates everything. [21]

[1]This means 'since an *abhāva* (= *dhavṁsābhāva*) is some effect.' This argument proceeds from answers to (a) and (b) in the preceding verses.

[2]*api* points to the *dṛṣṭānta* of a pot which is necessary for understanding the *vyāptivākya*. See note 4 below.

[3]*svahetusiddhi* means *svakāraṇasattā.*

[4]This is a form of *vyāptivākya*: *sarvaṁ kāryaṁ kāraṇapūrvakam.* One can understand: *yathā ghaṭādi*—cf. reference to *ghaṭādi* in verse 15 above.

Verse 21 answers the argument of the Mādhyamika regarding *sarvasya dhvaṁsa* (= *abhāva*) owing to the momentariness of everything. It raises two questions about the absence of everything: (i) Is it grasped by Direct Perception? or (ii) is it inferred? Consequently, the purport of the verse is that the Mādhyamika cannot make any argumentative proposition.

[5]The Śūnyavādin could not state a proposition (*pūrvam*) *asya sarvasya nāstitvam,* since the *pakṣa* (= *idaṁ sarvam*) was at that time not directly perceptible and therefore nothing could be predicated of it.

[6]This is *hetu* or *liṅga* in an *anumānavākya.* Where could one notice any characteristic of what did not exist? or, how could one postulate any characteristic of what did not exist? This means the *āśrayāsiddhi* and *svarūpāsiddhi* of the *hetu.*

[7]No example could be cited in respect of a proposition whose *pakṣa* itself is non-existent and therefore devoid of any property. Consequently, it would not help establish any conclusion (it would be *sādhyavikala*).

विज्ञानमात्रं यस्यापि जगदेतच्चराचरम् ॥
प्रतिज्ञाहेतुदृष्टान्तैर्ज्ञानं तेनापि दूष्यते ॥ २२ ॥

मानाभेदाच्च मेयस्य नाज्ञातार्थः प्रसिध्यति ॥
तादात्म्येऽपि न चेज्ज्ञातो मानात्कोऽतिशयो मतः ॥ २३ ॥

अज्ञाताधिगमं कुर्वन्मानं स्यात्सर्ववादिनाम् ॥
न चेच्छुक्तितमोजस्य ज्ञानस्यापि प्रमाणता ॥ २४ ॥

विज्ञानाव्यतिरेकित्वादसिद्धादेस्तथैव च ॥
प्रामाण्यवत्प्रसङ्गः स्यादप्रमात्वेऽपि ते ध्रुवम् ॥ २५ ॥

(Now, the inability of the Mādhyamika to make any proposition regarding *dhvaṁsa*, as pointed out in the previous verse, is stated of the Vijñānavādin also.)

Similarly (lit. also) the person for whom all this universe, moving and non-moving, is but Idea (*vijñāna*), would render his own knowledge faulty thanks to stating faulty (or false) enunciation, reason and example[1]. [22]

(Again,) owing to the non-difference (i.e. oneness) of the means of knowing with the object to be known, there does not become known (to a knower) any object that was unknown[2]. Also, if it were not known, even in case (one accepted) their non-difference, (it has to be pointed out as to) how what is produced or accepted is distinct[3] from the means of knowing. [23]

It is accepted among all thinkers that an authoritative means of knowing is what makes (the knower) know what was (earlier) unknown.[4] If this were not so, the knowledge produced from darkness (i.e. ignorance) about a shell would also be valid (i.e. authoritatively true). [24]

So also there would arise the contingency of accepting as the authoritative means of knowing what are not properly established as such,[5] in case they were not considered as distinct from Idea. [25]

[1]Verse 21 above pointed out three faults, viz. (i) *dharmyasiddhi*

in *pratijñāvākya*, (ii) *anāśraya hetu* and (iii) *dṛṣṭāntābhāva*, in the argument of the Mādhyamika. This is a statement that these same three faults occur in the argument of the Vijñānavādin. This is *jñānadoṣa*. Also there is reference to *hetvābhāsas*.

[2]This has a reference to *Pratyakṣa* 'Direct perception'. Any means of knowing is known to grasp what was not grasped before. Now, if knowledge and its objects are both Ideas, the means of knowing has no purpose to serve, i.e. it does not grasp what was not grasped.

[3]This is on the supposition that the means of knowing and the object of knowing are distinct—the latter has either (i) its unknownness removed or (ii) the character of having become known, produced by the means of knowing. The intention is to point out the impossibility of the function of any means of knowing in respect of an object of knowing which is the same as the knower.

[4]An argument of the Vijñānavādin could be: What makes something known is a means of knowing—not one which makes only an unknown known. This is answered away by pointing out that what produces invalid or false knowledge would also be considered as proper means of knowing.

[5]*asiddhādi* are *asiddha* (either *āśrayāsiddha* or *svarūpāsiddha*) and *viruddhahetus*.

अजमेकं स्वतःसिद्धं प्रत्यग्रूपमनन्यदृक् ॥
वस्त्वेवं चेदिहाभीष्टं किमर्थं साध्यतेऽपरम् ॥ २६ ॥

[Verses 26-31 are an argument regarding opposition to Advaita resulting from the statement of the existential character of both the cause and the effect.]

(An objector asks:) If in this Śāstra (of Advaita) you have accepted (lit. desired) (only) one existent which is unborn, self-established, having the form of the inner self (of an individual), and unlike any other (thing), for what purpose is anything else[1] being established? [26]

[1]This refers to the effect, viz. the *jagat*, which comprises

variety and would point to duality or absence of the uniqueness of the Brahman.

एवंभूतात्मसिद्ध्यर्थं कारणादि प्रसाध्यते ॥
उपायः सोऽवताराय तथा तज्ज्ञैश्च सूत्रितम् ॥ २७ ॥

Cause etc. are established (as existent) (only) with a view to establishing the Ātman of such nature; for, that is a means to introduce (the philosophical doctrine of the uniqueness of the Ātman)—so it is said (declared) by the knowers[1] of that. [27]

This verse is a reply to verse 26 above.

[1]Reference to Gauḍapāda in the plural is indication of Sureśvara's great regard for him. Cf. *Gauḍapādakārikā* 3.15:

mṛllohavisphuliṅgādyaiḥ sṛṣṭir yā coditānyathā|
upāyaḥ so 'vatārāya nāsti bhedaḥ kathaṁcana||

कारणादिनिषेधेन न चाद्वैतमभीप्सितम् ॥
ऐकात्म्यबोधमात्रेण निषेधस्याप्यपह्नवात् ॥ २८ ॥

(Only) by the rejection of the cause etc. is not established (lit. obtained) non-duality (of the Brahman), for, by the knowledge of its uniqueness alone (is secured) the rejection (of the cause and the effect etc. as real). [28]

So far, it has been pointed out that the existent pot etc. has an existent for its cause. How does it prove the non-duality of the Brahman? To answer this, the verse points out the uniqueness of the Brahman being established.

सत्तत्त्वकमिदं सर्वमिति संसाध्य यत्नतः ॥
तस्यापि संविन्मात्रेण पूर्णतैवोच्यते सतः ॥ २९ ॥

Having thus established with effort that all this is of the nature of (the existent)[1], the Śruti now declares the wholeness of that existent on account of only sentiency. [29]

[1]NKL reads the text as *sat-tattvakam* and not *sa-tattvakm* as in BUBV. According to this latter, the translation would be: 'all this that can be described as the cause and the effect etc. is but having the existent Ātman as its basic reality.' The reading in NKL seems better than that in BUBV, though we have rejected it.

सदेवागमतः सर्वं प्रत्यक्षाच्च सदीक्ष्यते ॥
अनुमानाच्च सत्सर्वं यथा तदधुनोच्यते ॥ ३० ॥

[This verse explains *anumeyatvāc ca*... (BUB p. 20)]

Now (i.e. hereafter) is stated (how) only the existent is all this, as declared by the Āgama (i.e. Śruti[1]), and also (as experienced) by direct perception as existent. Also, it is (proved) by inference as to how all (this) is that existent. [30]

[1]SP and NKL points to the Śruti text *mṛtyunaiva* in the BU and therefore the meaning of Āgama here cannot be 'tradition'.

अनुमेयं च सत्पूर्वं कारणं कार्यमेव च ॥
जगत्प्रसूतेस्तच्चेह प्रयोगेण प्रदर्श्यते ॥ ३१ ॥

[This verse explains *anumīyate* ca (BUB 1.2.1, p. 20)]

And both the cause and the effect can be inferred as preceded by the existent even (prior to) the creation of this universe; this is shown here (i.e. in what follows) by application (of the method of inference).

Verses 32-56 *prove the existential character of both the cause (viz. Brahman) before creation and its effect with reference to kāryasya hi... (BUB p.* 20).

विवादगोचरापन्नं सत्कारणमिदं भवेत् ॥
कार्यात्मकं मनोऽवादि कार्यत्वात्कटकुम्भवत् ॥ ३२ ॥

This (world) which has for its cause the existent is what has become the subject of dispute[1]. (And) *manas*, water etc.[2] of the nature of the cause[3], have been an effect comparable to a mat or a pot. [32]

[1]The word *dispute* affirms the nature of all effects as the *pakṣa*, viz. it is *sandigdhasādhyavat*, since, later, the word *kaṭakumbhavat* serves as the *dṛṣṭānta* in the proposed *prayoga*—cf. verse 31 above.

[2]Cf. BU 1.2.1 and 2.

[3]*kāryātmakam* puts *idam* (*jagat*) on par with *kaṭakumbha*.

हेतुमज्जनिमत्सर्वं कार्यत्वात्पटकुम्भवत् ॥
वियदादि च नः कार्यं तदप्येवं प्रतीयताम् ॥ ३३ ॥

All that has a birth has a (previously existing) cause, because it is of the nature of effect just like a piece of cloth or a pot.[1] May it be understood that the sky etc. is[2] for us effects, for that also[3] is like this[4]. [33]

[1]It is held by some that the world comes into existence, of itself, not from any cause (*svabhāvavāda*). This is here referred to.

[2]This is collective singular.

[3]Also can be understood for *samuccaya*: the first line refers to *anumāna* and the second to Āgama; refer to *antarikṣa* in BU 1.2.3—this (as also the translation) is according to the second alternative in SP.

[4]That is to say; *hetumat*.

The first alternative in SP (also in NKL) supplies *vibhaktatvāt* as the *hetu* for the affirmation in the second line; it means *svānyūnasattākabhedapratiyogitvāt* (NKL).

असत्कारणकं कार्यं तद्विनाश्यास्य जन्मतः ॥
सर्वं स्वहेतुमुन्मूल्य जायतेऽङ्कुरकुम्भवत् ॥ ३४ ॥

[This presents a counter-argument in the form of a *prayoga*.]
Every effect has a (previously) non-existent cause because it originates after having destroyed that; (for) all is born (only) after uprooting (i.e. destroying) its own cause in the same way as a sprout and/or a pot.[1] [34]

[1]It is argued thus: Being an effect should not be taken to mean that it has a cause necessarily existing before it. This is based on the common-place experience of the disappearance of a seed before the appearance of a sprout. The example of a sprout is not *sādhyavikala* 'deficient in respect of what is concluded'.

स्वकारणं चेदुत्साद्य कार्यं सर्वं प्रजायते ॥
तत्कारणविनाशाय तत्सूतेः प्राक्क्व ईर्यताम् ॥ ३५ ॥

स्वहेतूच्छित्तयेऽलं चेदजातमपि सद्यदि ॥
द्वयमप्यभ्युपेतं स्यान्न ह्यसद्धन्यतेऽसता ॥ ३६ ॥

[Verses 35-43 explain the meaning of *na* in *na mṛdādeḥ*.. (BUB p. 20). The next two verses (viz. 35-36) answer the counter-argument by pointing out how the example is *sādhyavikala.*]

If all effect[1] originated (only) after having destroyed its own cause, (then) let it be told as to where it was before its production for destroying its cause. [35]
If it were capable of destroying its own cause even while it had not originated and if it was then existent also, then you have accepted both of them (i.e. the cause and the effect) as existent before. Indeed, no non-existent can be destroyed by another non-existent. [36]

[1]This is collective singular.

विनाशस्यापि कार्यत्वात्सोऽपि सत्कारणो मम ॥
न चेत्कार्यो विनाशः स्यान्नाशोऽकार्येण नेष्यते ॥ ३७ ॥

Since destruction also is an effect, even[1] that has, in my opinion, an existent cause. If destruction were not to be considered as (something) to be effected, then (I should say) destruction by what is not an effect (itself) cannot be entertained.[2] [37]

[1]*api* shows that destruction has, like each of ***paṭa, kaṭa,*** and *kumbha* some existent cause.

[2]In other words what has not originated does not (or cannot) destroy.

स्वकारणविनाशाय सिद्धं वासिद्धमेव वा ॥
अङ्कुरादि मतं कार्यं नोभयत्रापि युज्यते ॥ ३८ ॥

If a sprout etc. is accepted (by you) as an effect, be it that the established (i.e. what has originated) or the non-established in respect of effecting the destruction of its own cause; both ways this[1] does not stand to reason. [38]

[1]'This' means the character of an effect as the destroyer of the cause.

सिद्धं चेत्कारणात्सिद्धमुपमर्दं विनैव तु ॥
उत्पन्नेन च तन्नाश उत्पन्नत्वादनर्थकः ॥ ३९ ॥

[The two ways mentioned in the previous verse are discussed in verses 39 and 40.]

If it is argued that what is established (i.e. has originated) has come into existence from its cause, without having destroyed it and the destruction of it is effected by the established effect, then (this) destruction would be purposeless[1] since the effect has already come into existence. [39]

[1]The reason is : The objector has posited the destruction of the seed etc. for purposes of the sprout's appearance (i.e. coming into existence).

उपमृद्नाति चेत्कार्यमथासिद्धं स्वकारणम् ॥
तत्कारणं कथं तत्स्यान्न चेत्तस्मात्प्रजायते ॥ ४० ॥

If it is said, 'an effect that is not established (i.e. has not originated) destroys its own cause', (then the question is:) how can that (cause) be its cause when it (viz. the effect) does not originate from it (viz. the cause)? [40]

उपमर्दोऽपि कार्यत्वात्किं न हन्यात्स्वकारणम् ॥
हन्तर्यसति हानोक्तिर्लक्ष्यते शिशुवक्तृका ॥ ४१ ॥

And, destruction also, being an effect, would it not destroy its own cause? (Indeed), in the absence of a destroyer, any statement about the destruction (of something) appears to have been made by a child (i.e. an ignorant person.) [41]

नंष्टृतन्त्रो विनाशोऽपि गन्तृतन्त्रा गतिर्यथा ॥
नास्तीह कश्चिद्धात्वर्थो यः स्वहेतुं विनाशयेत् ॥ ४२ ॥

Destruction also depends on some destroyer, in the same way as any movement depends on someone who moves. There is not here (i.e. in worldly language) a single meanning of any verbal root (viz. action) which would indicate the destruction of its agent[1]. [42]

[1]The meaning of any verbal root is some action which is performed by an agent and which therefore cannot destroy that agent.

निर्हेतुनाशसंव्याप्तेर्न स्यात्कुम्भजनिर्मृदः ॥
न बीजादग्निसंव्याप्तादङ्कुरोद्भूतिरीक्ष्यते ॥ ४३ ॥

It would not be possible that there is production of a pot from clay when there is pervasion (of that production) by the absence of the cause, viz. clay.[1] Indeed nowhere is seen the rise of a sprout from a seed which is pervaded (i.e. burnt) by fire.[2] [43]

[1]SP explains: This is as an answer to the Kṣaṇikavādin, according to whom everything is momentary. There, in his view, clay which is considered as the cause of a pot, is yet momentary. Consequently, he cannot say that a pot etc. comes into existence from nothing.

[2]This is an example to prove : *nāśavyāptāt kāraṇāt kāryānutpattiḥ.*

घटादेः कारणं पिण्ड इति नाभ्युपगम्यते ॥
मृदेव कारणं यस्मात्पिण्डादेरवगम्यते ॥ ४४ ॥

It is not accepted (by anyone) that the cause of a pot etc. is a lump etc.; (they hold) only clay as the cause since it is understood (to be existent) from (its form as a lump). [44]

यदेव कारणं मानैरिह साक्षाद्विनिश्चितम् ॥
तदेवोत्तरकार्येषु न कार्यं कारणं मितेः ॥ ४५ ॥

[This is to explain the second line of the preceding verse.]

Whatever cause, which is established here[1] by various means of knowing[2] (only) clearly[3], is itself (the cause) in respect of the later effects. (Indeed) it can be argued that an effect is not the cause of (any other effect of the same cause), thanks to (proper) way of knowing.[4] [45]

[1]That is to say; in respect of a lump (of clay) etc. which is the first form of an effect.

[2]These are: *anvaya*, *vyatireka*, *anusaṁdhāna* and *pratyaya*.

[3]That is to say; by direct perception, in the first instance.

[4]Form of the material cause (of clay) does not remain permanent and also that form, being an effect itself, does not persist in the effect; this is (i) *anvaya* of clay in a pot, and (ii) *anavasthāna* (non-existence) of the lump etc. in the pot etc. *miti* is *māna* = *jñāna*.

विनाशोऽतिशयः कश्चिद्यदि पिण्डादिवन्मतः ॥
प्रत्यक्षात्तद्द्वयं सत्स्यान्नो चेदस्तु ध्रुवो घटः ॥ ४६ ॥

If it was held that destruction of clay is some excellence of it just like the lump etc., then, since both of them (viz. destruction and clay), being directly perceptible, would be (ever) existent.[1] (And) if (it were) not so[2], (then) let the pot be (considered as) permanent.[3] [46]

[1]The argument in this verse proceeds to refute a possible

counter-objection. Like the lump of clay (i.e. a form of it), clay also is liable to destruction. This objection entails a doubt whether destruction of clay is some excellence (i.e. modification) of it. The answer is: Excellence of a thing and the thing must both be directly perceptible; therefore, clay and its so-called excellence, viz. destruction, must also be directly perceptible and consequently ever-obtaining.

[2]This is another part of the doubt, viz. destruction is not any excellence of clay, it is different from it.

[3]This is so, because destruction (which is *abhāva*, i.e. non-existence) is in no way related to the pot which is an existential entity. The pot is clearly an effect and a form of clay. And further, the nature of destruction is thus not in any way ascertained.

क्रिया वा तत्फलं वा स्याद्वस्त्वन्तरमथापि वा ॥
नाशोऽथ वा न किंचित्स्यात्सत्त्वं नैवमपोद्यते ॥ ४७ ॥

Or, whatever be (the nature of) destruction (e.g. of clay), either some action or the effect of the same something distinct from it or some non-entity, its existence cannot be declined. [47]

The nature of destruction could be understood in any of the four ways, but that (viz. the nature of destruction) would not establish the non-existence of an existent, which still continues to exist.

क्रियाप्यस्ति फलं चास्ति तद्वद्वस्त्वन्तरं च सत् ॥
अथ नाशोऽपि नैवास्ति तं विना सदिदं जगत् ॥ ४८ ॥

[The second line of the preceding verse is explained here.]

Now destruction may be some action or some result (or modification) or some thing other (than an existent e.g. clay) or some non-entity. Even then this universe is existent despite its absence.[1] [48]

[1]This is to be explained thus: If destruction is some action, the agent of the action has to be declared as existent and this

would not negate the existential character of a thing like clay. If it is some result (or modification), then what has undergone this change has to be considered as an existent. If it is another (existential) thing, it does not affect the nature of things like clay etc. Being a non-entity also, it does not affect the status of the same.

सन्नेव नाशोऽपीष्टश्चेत्सत्सता न विरुध्यते ॥
ऐकात्म्येऽपि विरोधश्चेन्नाशो नाशेऽपि शङ्कचते ॥ ४६ ॥

If one were to accept destruction also as an existent, then (it has to be pointed out) the existent (clay) is not opposed (i.e. disproved as existent) by (another) existent (viz. destruction). And, if one were to say that even there is unity of nature (of the two, viz. destruction and clay), then (it would mean that) one would have to doubt that there is destruction (in the case) of destruction also. [49]

The last line implies that, like destruction of clay, there can be destruction of destruction also. Thus, the nature of destruction being unestablished, clay has to be declared as an existent.

पिण्डादिना विनापीदं मृदादेः केवलादपि ॥
घटाद्युत्पद्यमानं तु कार्यं दृष्टमतो ध्रुवम् ॥ ५० ॥
मृदाद्येव ततो ग्राह्यं करणं ह्यन्वयान्मृदः ॥
कार्यमेव तु पिण्डादि तस्य कार्येष्वनन्वयात् ॥ ५१ ॥

[Verse 50 is an amplification of the idea in verse 45. Verse 51 gives the outcome of the argument of verse 50.]

It is invariably seen that the effect, a pot etc. is produced, even without (the form of) a lump (of clay) but from clay alone (i.e. clay having no form). Therefore, it (i.e. clay) is ever existent. [50]

Therefore,[1] only clay etc. has to be accepted as the cause, indeed from its continued existence (in the effect, viz. pot). As against this (*tu*), the (form of a) lump etc. is but an effect, for it does not continue to exist in the effect. [51]

Earlier, in the explanation of *miti* in verse 45, reference was made to *anvayavyatirekasaṁbandha*. That is explained here. *piṇḍādinā* etc. is the amplification of *asati api*.. (BUB p. 20). The lines *dhruvam* etc. are the explanation of *tasmān na*.. (BUB p. 20).

[1]'Therefore' has reference to 'it is invariably *seen*'.

विरुद्धानेककार्याणां युगपज्जन्म नेष्यते ॥
एकस्मात्कारणात्तस्मात्पिण्डाभावे घटोद्भवः ॥ ५२ ॥

It is not accepted that there is simultaneous production (lit. birth) of many mutually opposed effects from one single cause. Therefore, there is production of a pot (even) while there is absence of (the form) of a lump. [52]

This is a comment *sarvaṁ hi kāraṇam*.. (BUB p. 20). This is to explain why there does not originate a pot together with a lump which forms from clay. True, the lump is clay, but it is an effect of clay, a pot is not the effect of the lump.

पिण्डादिव्यतिरेकेण कारणानुपलब्धितः ॥
असत्त्वं चेन्मृदादेः स्यान्न मानानुपपत्तितः ॥ ५३ ॥

If one were to argue: Since one does not find the cause (as existent) apart from lump etc., therefore clay etc. have non-existence.[1] (The answer is:) No, that is not so, because there is invalidity of that means of knowing.[2] [53]

[1]The objector means to add 'and therefore clay etc. is not the cause of a pot etc.'

[2]This means: The lump etc. cannot form without the presence (or existence) of clay etc. (*mṛdādyanugatava*). Therefore, the reasoning of the objector stands invalid.

पिण्डादिव्यतिरेकेण यदि मानं भवेत्ततः ॥
मृदादि कारणं लब्धं न मानं स्यान्मृदा विना ॥ ५४ ॥

पिण्डादिव्यतिरेकेण पिण्डादाविव चेत्प्रमा ॥
सिद्धं कारणमेवं स्यान्न मा मेयं विना यतः ॥ ५५ ॥

[This explains further what is stated in the previous verse.]

If (one were to say: The argument of the Vedāntin appears to be that) the means of knowing (the existent cause) obtains even apart from (i.e. in the absence of) a lump[1] etc., then (in that case, we answer that) there does obtain clay etc. as the cause; (for) there would not obtain any means (of knowing, i.e. ascertaining, the cause) in the absence of clay.[2] [54]

If (one were to say:) As in (the absence of) a lump (of clay) etc. there results the knowledge of the cause, apart from the lump,[3] then (one has to declare that the existence of) the cause is proved this way (also); for, there results no knowledge in the absence of an object of knowledge.[4] [55]

[1]SP points out the argument of the objector thus: Clay and the form of a lump (of that clay) co-exist. Therefore, the form being destroyed, clay also must be said to cease to exist.

[2]The Siddhāntin answers that the *anugatatva* 'continued existence' of clay etc. decides the conclusion. This is stated by *vyatireka* mode of answer.

[3]The objector has this in mind: Clay (not in the form of a lump) and a lump of it cannot easily be distinguished from each other, therefore, it is difficult to say that the clay, which continues to exist even in the absence of the form of a lump, is the cause of a pot.

[4]The objector's argument is not really any objection. The knowledge of the continued existence of the clay etc. is the reason to prove it as the cause of the existing pot. A second proposition about the knowledge and its means points to this.

असाधारणरूपेषु व्यावृत्तेष्वितरेतरम् ॥
बहुष्वेकं यदाभाति प्रत्यक्षं कारणं तु तत् ॥ ५६ ॥

The one, that is directly perceptible in those many (of its forms), each of which has a distinct form and gets destroyed (lit. disappears) (in the process of the creation of some effect), is the cause.[1] [56]

[1]Translation follows the latter of the two alternative explanations given by SP. The former alternative is: They recognize that as the cause of some effect which is preceded by those many forms that have mutually differed and ceased to exist. Of course, there is very little material difference between these two.

In verses 57-73, *the topic pertains to the doubt about the perception of continued existence of something which results from its similarity with what could be the real cause.*

सादृश्यादन्वयभ्रान्तिस्तन्निवृत्तावपीति चेत् ॥
नैवं पिण्डस्थदृष्टानां घटादावपि दर्शनात् ॥ ५७ ॥

If one were to hold that, there would be on the part of one an error as regards the continued existence (of the cause in what is held as its effect) on account of the similarity of any or (many of its so-called products with it) even when they have (gradually) ceased to exist (when the effect exists), then (we say:) This is not so[1], since the parts (of clay etc.) which are seen in its various forms are noticed even in the pot etc. [57]

[1]This is denial of *bhrānti* 'error', for our experience of a clay-pot is thus; 'this is a pot of clay'. This experience does not get stultified as any *bhrānti* does.

प्रत्यभिज्ञायमानेऽर्थे तदेवेदमिति ध्रुवे ॥
लिङ्गमाभासतामेति प्रत्यक्षार्थविरुद्धमित् ॥ ५८ ॥

In the object (viz. the pot) that is being recognized as 'this is the same as that', while that object has remained unchanged, (what the objector holds as) the cause becomes apparently perceptible in the form (only) (to him)[1] but this (his) knowledge is opposed to the directly perceived object.[2] [58]

[1]This is an argument of the Kṣaṇikavādin. He holds that all these so-called existent objects are but momentary even like a

lamp that illumines its surrounding only for a while (i.e. for a moment). Therefore, what is considered as the experience of the continued existence of clay etc. (*anvayadṛṣṭi*) is positively an error. This is actually some kind of inference of the oneness (or, the continuance) of the cause.

[2]This refers to the recognition of clay etc. In the momentary appearances of the objects of the Kṣaṇikavādin's knowledge, there is never such recognition. There is thus opposition of the objector's *anumāna* and the (*pratyabhijñā*) *pratyakṣa* of the Siddhāntin.

विरुद्धाव्यभिचारित्वं न च प्रत्यक्षलिङ्गयोः ॥
प्रत्यक्षापाश्रयान्नित्यं नानपेक्षं तदक्षवत् ॥ ॥ ५६ ॥

[A further argument in respect of *anumāna* in the face of *pratyakṣa* or (even) *pratyabhijñā*.]

And between Direct Perception and Inference[1], there is not any invariable opposition[2], for, it (*liṅga*) ever rests on Direct Perception; it is not independent (i.e. without any expectation of Direct Perception[3]). [59]

[1]*liṅga* stands for *anumāna*. Cf. also the preceding verse.
[2]This is explained in the first line of the next verse.
[3]*akṣa* = *pratyakṣa* 'Direct Perception'.

विरुद्धाव्यभिचारित्वं समानवलयोर्यतः ॥
दृष्टं सर्वत्र लोकेऽस्मिन्न तु सिंहशृगालयोः ॥ ६० ॥

(And also) because the relation of being mutually opposed invariably (can) obtain (only) between two reasons of equal strength.[1] This is seen everywhere in this world, but it (i.e. such invariable opposition) is not noticed to exist between a lion and a fox (which are of unequal strength).[2] [60]

Translation uses the word reasons for conveying the idea of *hetu* in *Anumāna*.

NKL clarifies the meaning of *viruddhāvyabhicāritva*; it consists in invariable association of something with what is opposed to it. Cf. the well-known idea expressed in the Nibandhas belonging to Prācina Nyāya: *viruddhārthadvayabodhakahetvoḥ prayoge satpratipakṣāparaparyāyatayā 'viruddhāvyabhicārī' iti vyavahāraḥ*. Here *Liṅga* = *Anumāna* leads to the knowledge that there is no existent cause of a *ghaṭa*, and, as opposed to it, *Pratyakṣa* leads to the knowledge that the existent clay is its cause. Thus, the two means of knowing lead to *sādhyābhāva* and *sādhya* both. Therefore, either of these two means of knowing (i.e. two *hetus*) can be called *satpratipakṣa* 'inconclusive or ambiguous' *hetus*. The argument in this verse is based on the dependence of *Anumāna* on *Pratyakṣa*. The continued presence of clay, therefore, shows the invalidity of the *Anumāna* so-called.

[1]This explains the inequality (i.e. degree of adequacy) of the two *hetus* mentioned in the preceding verse. The two alleged *hetus* (i.e. the mutually opposed *Pratyakṣa* and *Liṅga*) are not equally strong.

[2]The statement in the first line is supported by citing a similar example from common life. There can be opposition worth the name between the two lions or two foxes, but not between a lion and a fox.

क्षणिकत्वे च भावानां प्रत्यभिज्ञाद्यसंभवः ॥
न ह्यन्यदृष्टं वस्त्वन्यैः प्रत्यभिज्ञायते क्वचित् ॥ ६१ ॥

[One more argument against *kṣaṇikatva*; *pratyabhijñā* etc. would be impossible.]

> In case one holds that things of existence are momentary, there would be impossibility of recognition (of those things) etc.[1] (on the part of the onlookers of those things). Indeed, a thing which is seen by someone is not recognized by any other person.[2] [61]

[1]SP explains *ādi* 'etc.' on the basis of BS 3.2.9: *sa eva tu karmānusmṛtiśabdavidhibhyaḥ* which refers to some action that had remained incomplete at an earlier moment (or on an earlier day) to re-

collection or remembrance of what was seen or done earlier and also to scriptural passages such as BU 4.3.16 and CU 6.9.3. and 8.3.2. NKL follows suit. Better, however, refer to BS 2.2.25 which refutes the Buddhist's notion of momentariness of things (and also of knowers of them).

[2]This implies that the unity of a seer is denied by the Kṣaṇikavādin—this is amplified in the next verse.

क्षणिकं चेदिदं सर्वं प्रत्यभिज्ञाप्रमाणकम् ॥
अन्यतद्बुद्ध्यपेक्षत्वं तद्बुद्धेर्वः प्रसज्यते ॥ ६२ ॥

If all this, which has recognition as the means of knowing it, is (held by the Kṣaṇikavādin as) momentary, then he[1] will have to face the contingency of accepting that it (i.e. recognition of some object) is dependent on the knowledge (of it on the part) of another. [62]

[1]'He' refers to the Kṣaṇikavādin, who is directly addressed in the verse.

इदं क्षणिकमित्येतत्क्षणिकत्वे न सिध्यति ॥
इदंक्षणिकताबुद्ध्योर्भिन्नाधिकरणत्वतः ॥ ६३ ॥

[This verse states the reason why momentariness of things etc. cannot hold.]

(Further) in the view that everthing is momentary the proposition 'this is momentary' does not get established, because the knowledge 'this one' and 'momentariness' of (it) belong to two different substrata[1]. [63]

[1]Substrata:

(a) (reference to cognisers, i.e. individuals): This proposition, 'This is momentary' is said to imply the non-momentariness of the one who makes it, for one requires to live two moments to have two cognitions of (i) this, and (ii) its characteristic momentariness. If this implication is not accepted, it would mean two cognisers for the two cognitions which turn into one cognition.

And already, the second line of the 61st verse has pointed out the impossibility of such a happening in the case of a cogniser, viz. the second cogniser (of momentariness).

(b) (reference to cognitions, i.e. time): (a) entails that there are two cognitions (let us say, on the part of even one cogniser (and not two of them). And these two cognitions cannot obtain in just one moment—there would be two moments necessary. Consequently, there cannot be the cognition of this form: 'This is momentary.' !

अज्ञातं ज्ञायते यस्य तथाजातं च जायते ॥
प्रत्यभिज्ञामृते तस्य प्रतिज्ञार्थो न सिध्यति ॥ ६४ ॥

[This verse shows how even the Kṣaṇikavādin has to accept recognition as a means of knowing.]

For him, in whose opinion what was not known (before) becomes known and what was not born becomes born, the thing enunciated (i.e. mentioned as the subject of any of the propositions) cannot get established, unless it is recognised. [64]

To say, 'This was not and is (now) born' or 'This was unknown and is (now) known' implies two moments for the one who says it. That should force the Kṣaṇikavādin to accept recognition as a proper/authoritative means of knowing.

अनवस्था च दुर्वारा ह्यविश्वासश्च जायते ॥
मृषात्वात्सर्वबुद्धीनां न क्वचिन्निश्चितिर्भवेत् ॥ ६५ ॥

(If the holder of the view of momentariness says that, 'we do not say: an unknown is known or an unborn is born',[1] then) there would follow inevitable *infinite regress* and further there would arise (among the people) want of faith (in the doctrine of momentariness). (Thus) on account of all knowledges (in that system or view) being false[2] (i.e. invalid), there would not be any definite decision. [65]

[1]This would mean 'what is (already) known is being known' or 'what is (already) born is being born'. Who could believe this as a reasonable talk?

[2]All statements made by the Kṣaṇikavādin will be held unauthoritative. The purport of philosophical inquiry would thus be defeated !

संबन्धानुपपत्तिश्च तदिदंज्ञानयोर्ध्रुवम् ॥
संबन्धकर्तर्यसति न च सादृश्यसंश्रयात् ॥ ६६ ॥

And certainly that relation between the two knowledges of that and of this would be unreasonable (or invalid), when there does not exist one who would relate them[1]. And also, (that relation could not obtain) on the support of similarity[2] (between that and this). [66]

This argument proceeds from the fact that the statement of the cognition 'This is that' would require two moments of time or two places as the substratum of the cognition. Alternatively, it would require at least the knowledge of the similarity between this, and that and this knowledge would require the continued existence of the knower.

[1]This means 'who is the knower of the relation.'
[2]This is explained in the next verse.

ध्वंसिनोरिव सादृश्यं स्थायिनोरपि नेष्यते ॥
ग्राहकेऽसति तद्भिन्ने बुद्धीनां चैकरूपतः ॥ ६७ ॥

That there is similarity is not accepted in the case of two objects that continue to exist as in the case of those which get destroyed (in a moment) when there is not a perceiver of them who is different from the two.[1] (This is so) also because the knowledges of two (or more) similar objects are held to be of but one form. [67]

[1]Translation follows the reading *tadbhinne* whose variant reading *tad-bhitteḥ* is supported by NKL. In that case, the word *tad-*

bhitti means difference between the two knowers of the two. SP remarks that the difference in the reading does not change the conclusion. The thought is: There is need of but one knower who continues to live (at least) the two moments of the cognition of two similar things, whether they are momentary or permanent. *tadbhitti* means difference between two knowers of the two similar objects. This causes the difficulty: Similarity cannot be spoken of, in case there are two different cognitions of two different knowers! Cf. *aikyabuddher bhrāntitvabhaṅgena bhāveṣu kṣaṇitvam abhāṅkṣīt*—the introductory remark in SP on the next verse.

नाशभेदविरुद्धार्थप्रमेये च व्यवस्थिते ॥
प्रत्यर्थिनि हि प्रत्यक्षे तद्विरुद्धः कुतोऽमितेः ॥ ६८ ॥

[This verse states yet another argument against *kṣaṇikatva.*]

When there exists thus an object of knowledge which is opposed (in nature) to destruction or discreteness (from one another) and (further) Direct Perception is an opponent (of the two[1]), how could there be what is opposed to that[2]?—because there is (really) the absence of any (other) means of the knowledge (of the two). [68]

Here, the verse refers to the Buddhist view of *nirvikalpaka pratyakṣa. nirvikalpakapratyakṣa* is opposed to destruction etc., it grasps only what exists. Yet this also does not prove momentariness of objects (NKL).

Translation follows the reading adopted by SP which reads: *amiter iti padacchedaḥ*. However, NKL reads *kutaḥ miteḥ*. Accordingly, translation of the second line would be: Whence, i.e. by what means could there be... (*kasmān mānād ityarthaḥ*) (NKL).

[1]These are: destruction of what is considered as the antecedent, the cause, and discreteness of two cognitions which form the basis of *sādṛśya*.

[2]'That' refers to Direct Perception.

अनुत्पन्नोत्पित्सूत्पन्नोऽनष्टो नाशादिकृत्तथा ॥
एवमष्टक्षणावस्थो भावोऽवश्यं त्वयेष्यते ॥ ६९ ॥

[Yet another argument about self-contradiction in the view of the Kṣaṇikavādin.]

(Do remember) even you have necessarily to accept that a thing exists for eight moments, for, (in your view) it is (i) not produced, (ii) wanting to be produced, (iii) being produced, (iv) produced, (v) not-destroyed, i.e. existent, (vi) wanting to destroy (itself), (vii) destroyer[1] (of itself), and (viii) destroyed.[2] [69]

[1]This stands for *nāṣakṛt*. It is difficult to say what *ādi* in *nāśādikṛt* means.

[2]This is comparable to six modifications of a thing (*ṣaṭ bhāvavikāras*) mentioned in *Nirukta* 1.2: *jāyate*, *asti*, *vardhate*, *pariṇamati*, *apakṣīyate*, *vinaśyati*.

अन्योन्याविषयत्वे तु कुतः सादृश्यधीरियम् ॥
सदृशार्थं विनैवेयं क्लृप्ता सादृश्यधीर्यदि ॥ ७० ॥

[So far, Sureśvara has explained the meaning only of *na* in *na tadidaṁbuddhyaḥ* ... (BUB p. 22). Now he explains the remaining part of the statement.]

In the first instance[1], since you hold that (in a cognition of similarity, the two similar objects) do not grasp each other[2], whence[3] does this knowledge of similarity (arise) then? And, (you entertain that), if there is this knowledge of similarity, then (you have entertained that, viz. the notion of that knowledge) even without the existence of similar objects[3]. [70]

The Buddhists hold that knowledge occurs of itself (i.e. it is *svayaṁvedya*). Therefore, the question arises as to who grasps the similarity between 'this' and 'that'. The notion of *svayaṁvedyatva* stands therefore in the need of explanation of the problem: Do they, i.e. this and that, grasp each other as similar? It cannot be answered? Therefore, the question: 'Who grasps this similarity?' remains unanswered.

[1]This is the meaning of *tāvat*.

[2]It literally means 'do not have the each other as the object of its knowing.'

[3]If both this and that are momentary then the notion of the knowledge of similarity between themselves on the part of each of them is baseless. This is so, because similarity can be grasped only when both the subject and the object co-exist and are not *svayaṁvedya*.

मृगाम्बुधीवन्मिथ्यात्वं स्यादेवं तदिदंधियोः ॥
असद्विषयतैवेह सर्वासामपि चेद्धियाम् ॥ ७१ ॥

नैवं बुद्धेरपि तथा ह्यसद्विषयता भवेत् ॥
अस्त्वेवं सर्वबुद्धीनां मृषात्वमिति चेन्मतम् ॥ ७२ ॥

नैवं स्यात्सर्वबुद्धीनां मृषात्वे मित्यसंभवात् ॥
कारणस्यास्तिता तस्मात्सिद्धा कार्योद्भवात्पुरा ॥ ७३ ॥

[This is the refutation of the three Buddhist schools: In line 1 of verse 71, the Bāhyārthavādins; line 2 of verse 71 and line 1 of verse 72, the Vijñānavādin; and the line 2 of verse 72 and line 1 of verse 73; the Śūnyavādin—finally, line 2 of verse 73 states the Siddhānta.]

Thus[1], there would be two false knowledges: (i) of this and (ii) of that exactly as that of a mirage[2]. (If it is said;) let all knowledges have (only) non-existent objects, [71]

this is not so, for in respect of momentary knowledge also, the situation would be that there is a non-existent object of knowledge. If it were held that all knowledges are but false, [72]

this would not be so, because there would then be no possibility of any knowledge. Thereby is established the existence of the cause before the production of the effect. [73]

[1]It means to say: It follows from the above argument.

[2]The mistake in respect of a mirage lies in wrongly apprehending water in the place of thin air.

In verses 74-107 Sureśvara has undertaken to prove the previous existence of the cause and the effect before the latter came to be produced. In the earlier portion, he explained the existence of the cause; now, he explains how the effect (also) existed. This is an explanation of kāryasya cābhivyaktiliṅgatvāta .. (BUB p. 22).

कार्यस्यापि यथाऽस्तित्वं तथेदानीं प्रपञ्च्यते ॥
सत्त्वपूर्वमिदं कार्यं तमोन्तस्थघटादिवत् ॥
तस्याभिव्यक्तिधर्मत्वादन्यथा स्यान्नृशृङ्गवत् ॥ ७४ ॥

Now is explained in detail[1] how there is existence of the effect. This[2] effect has existence (even) before (it is produced) like that of a pot which remains in darkness,[3] for it has the characteristic of being revealed[4]. If this were not so, it would be like the (never existing) horns of a human being. [74]

[1]The denominative root *prapañcaya-* means 'to explain in detail'.

[2]The word *idam* refers to what is directly perceptible, or, being revealed as the so-called effect.

[3]The example a pot that was covered in darkness before it came to be noticed is an alternative exposition of *abhivyaktidharmatvāt* which SP has explained as *sammatābhivyaktavad abhivyaktatvāt (anumeyam)*.

[4]SP paraphrases: *abhivyajyamānatvāt.*

सत्यामपि च सामग्र्यां वन्ध्यापुत्राद्यसत्त्वतः ॥
विज्ञानालम्बनत्वं नो न कदाचित्प्रपद्यते ॥ ७५ ॥

Even while there exist the means[1] of knowing, the son of a barren woman etc.[2], they owing to their non-existence (are not seen); but (in respect of the knowledge of the cause and its effect) it does not stand to reason (to say that) there is no basis for knowing (these)[3]. [75]

[1]That is to say, eye, light etc.

[2]The word *ādi* refers to *nṛśṛṅga*, *khapuṣpa*, and other such falsely conceived existents (!).

[3]Idea (*vijñāna*) is the basis for knowing them.

सर्वं सदेव चेदिष्टमुपलभ्येत ते सदा ॥
सामग्र्यां घटवत्सत्यां सर्वं सद्वादिनो ध्रुवम् ॥ ७६ ॥

[This is an objection.]

(One might object): If you accept that all this (world of effects, viz. objects of knowledge) ever obtains as existent, then, so long as there exist the means of knowing (the same), in the same way as a pot, everything would be for the Siddhāntin invariably existent. [76]

न विद्यमानमात्रेण ह्यभिव्यक्तिरपीष्यते ॥
सदेव वस्त्वभिव्यक्तं च तथाऽव्यक्तं लक्ष्यते ॥ ७७ ॥

[This is the answer to the objection in the previous verse.]

(We say:) (No, it is not so.) Indeed[1] we do not accept even[2] manifestation (of an object as previously existent) by its mere existence; (in our opinion); an existent object is noticed to become manifest and also (that which can remain) unmanifest.[3] [77]

This argument is in answer to two doubts: (1) Whether being existent at this moment is alone the basis of the ever existence of the cause; and (ii) whether it is mere existence of the means of knowing it.

[1]The word *hi* is paraphrased by SP thus: Accepting that all are ever existent (read: *sarvasammatidyotanārtho hiśabdaḥ*).

[2]The word 'etc.' refers to the existent object's use in human dealings.

[3]Only existent can manifest itself in various forms (*āvirbhāva*) or withdraw (i.e. conceal) some (or all) of its forms (*tirodhāna*).

अङ्गीकर्तव्यमेतच्च भवद्भिरविशङ्कितैः ॥
न चेद्वः सर्वसिद्धान्तो नश्येत्सैकतकूपवत् ॥ ७८ ॥

And this view is to be accepted by you without having any doubt.[1] If you do not do so, your entire doctrine would topple down (lit. get destroyed) like a well of sand.[2] [78]

[1]The argument is: An effect cannot be said to exist while all the factors which cause it are noticeable, since (according to the Naiyāyika) there is a relation between the two as the antecedent and that which follows it. This sets aside the possibility that only a previously existent effect comes to get manifested.

[2]The Naiyāyika is a realist and, therefore, by accepting what is said in the previous line, he has to give up realism and accept the unreality (or, non-existence) of an effect—that is, he would be reduced to the position of a Kṣaṇikavādin.

प्रमाणव्यतिरेकेण प्रमेयोऽर्थो भवन्भवेत् ॥
मानादव्यतिरेके हि मानमेयौ न सिध्यतः ॥ ७९ ॥

An object of knowledge exists (only if it exists) apart from the one who knows (it)[1]; (and) if the knower were not apart from the means of knowing, it would not be possible to hold that there exists knowledge and the means of knowing.[2] [79]

The verse has a basis in the Vijñānavādin's view that both the knowledge (of an object) and the object of knowledge are but Ideas and it answers in two separate lines, two questions: (i) Should one include knowledge in the means of knowing? and (ii) Should one include the means of knowing in knowledge?

[1]This is the answer to the first question. It is possible to say that there is some object of knowing, if it were different from some knower of it.

[2]This is the answer to the second question. One cannot posit two entities as knowledge and the means to it, if they were but one idea.

कारणस्यापि नास्तित्वं कार्यासत्त्वे प्रसज्यते ॥
न हि कार्यमनाश्रित्य कारणं जगतीक्ष्यते ॥ ८० ॥

And, further, in case one accepted the non-existence of an effect (before its effect was produced), there would follow the contingency that the cause also did not exist, for indeed nowhere in the universe is seen any cause which is not related to an effect. [80]

This has a reference to the Asatkāryavāda of the Naiyāyikas, who hold that an effect did not exist before its production. There are two possibilities as to how this is so: (i) There never existed any effect, and (ii) there were no means of its production. The second question only has to be answered. This is done in this verse. The second line points out how cause and effect are only inter-related and, therefore, one cannot exist in the absence of the other.

सत्तामात्रेण किं कार्यंसमवाय्यादि कारणम् ॥
साधयेद्व्यापृतं वेदं तथाऽपीष्टं न सिध्यति ॥ ८१ ॥

[*The edition of NKL correctly reads samavāyyādi and kāraṇam as two words.*]

[Up to verse 80 Sureśvara refuted Satkāryavāda represented by the Tārkika and some Buddhists who also are good logicians. Now, verse 81-87 are *anukta* portion in the comments of Śaṅkara, but implied by him.]

(The question is:) Is it that causes, beginning with the invariable antecedent cause[1], produce any effect by mere existence of them? or (would they produce that), being active[2]? (Whatever be it), the desired[3] (absence of relation between the cause and the effect) does not get established. [81]

There are two possibilities which would be thought by the Tārkikas; viz. (i) the cause does not operate, yet it produces the effect by its mere existence; and (ii) the cause operates and then produces the effect. In verses 81 onwards, Sureśvara refutes Ārambhavāda of the Tārkika.

[1]The Tārkika enunciates three causes, *samavāyi*, *asamavāyi* and *nimitta*.

[2]*vyāpṛtaṁ vā* implies *avyāpṛtam*; this latter is the basis for verse 85.

[3]The Tārkika wants to establish the absence of the effect.

सत्तामात्रेण चेत्कुर्यात्कारणत्रितयं तदा ॥
कार्योत्पत्तिस्थितिलयाः प्राप्नुयुर्युगपत्सदा ॥ ८२ ॥

अविशेषाच्च सत्तायाः सर्वतः सर्वसंभवः ॥
सर्व एव न संसिध्येद्व्यवहारश्च लौकिकः ॥ ८३ ॥

त्रीण्येव कारणानीति निष्फलावधृतिर्भवेत् ॥
यथा त्रयं तथा सर्वं सत्तया किं न कारणम् ॥ ८४ ॥

If the three causes would produce effects (i.e. results) by their mere existence, then (i.e. in that case) production, existence and merger of effects would ever be occurring (lit. obtaining) simultaneously[1]. [82]

And (in this case), since (mere) existence (of the causes) has not undergone any change,[2] there would be the possibility of the production of all (kinds of) things from all other things and consequently all the worldly dealings of (cause and effect) would not be possible).[3] [83]

(Furthermore) (the emphatic) assertion (i.e. enunciation) that there are only three causes would be meaningless. As you accept the three causes as mere existent (and responsible for the production of effects), why would you not accept (i.e. mention) that all things can together be the cause by their mere existence?[4] [84]

[1]This refers to the impossibility of making one cause from another.

[2]This means that each of them would remain as some existent and would be incapable of giving rise to any effect (that is change). There would be these causes existing in mere name—and not meaningfully so !

[3]NKL points out how one, who is desirous of obtaining oil, would not avoid using milk as the material for producing oil.

[4]This has reference to the statement *sarvataḥ sarvasambhavaḥ* in verse 83.

संभूय कार्यं कुर्याच्चेत्कारणत्रितयं तदा ॥
मेलनस्यापि कार्यत्वात्कथं तत्स्यात्त्रयं विना ॥ ८५ ॥

If the three causes would operate together[1] (i.e. produce an effect), then their coming together[2] also being an effect, (one should have to explain) how that would be possible without the three. [85]

[1]See note 4 under verse 81 above.

[2]A variant reading is noted in NKL: *melaka* for *melana*. But this reading does not seem in any way significant. The text of NKL accepts *melaka*. In case the reading of NKL is accepted, the *melaka* should be distinct from the three causes, either related or unrelated to the three causes. But the words *melakasyāpi kāryatvāt* do not get explained satisfactorily. And NKL is silent about the same !

कारणत्रितये नाथ एकैकस्य प्रसिध्यति ॥
तस्य तस्य तथैवेति सानवस्था प्रसज्यते ॥ ८६ ॥

Also the (operation) of any one among the (group of the) three causes cannot stand to reason (i.e. cannot produce an effect), (for), then it would each require in the same way (an operator bringing the three causes together) (and) thus[1] there would result *infinite regress*. [86]

SP explains that the absence of Saṁdhi in *nātha ekaikasya* is purely the author's choice: *vivakṣito hi saṁdhir bhavatiti manyate*. The edition of NKL reads: *kāraṇatritayeṇātha*. Translation, in that case, would be difficult. Translation here follows the AnSS text. Further, SP shows *atho* as a variant for *atha* and points out that it would be the sense of *api ca*.

The argument in this verse would set aside the Ārambhavāda.

[1]SP points out that *sā anavasthā* 'such *infinite regress*' would follow also if Kṣaṇikavāda is accepted.

वस्तुनः सदसत्त्वाय ह्यभिव्यक्त्येकहेतुतः ॥
ऐश्वर्यं न प्रमाणस्य सत्त्वं वस्तुबलाद्यतः ॥ ८७ ॥

The means of knowing does not indeed have any strength (i.e. capacity) for (establishing) the existence or non-existence of a thing, because it is only the cause of revealing the thing (and also) because the existence (of a thing gets established) in its own right.[1] [87]

[1]SP points to the instance of a hidden treasure, which is not seen by one and yet exists in its own right. This sets aside a possible argument: *yad upalabhyate tad eva sat* 'only peceptible is existent'.

द्वैविध्यादावृतेः कार्यं नेक्षते तेन संवृतम् ॥
लब्धात्मकस्य कुड्यादि प्राक्सूतेः कारणावृतिः ॥ ८८ ॥

[Upto verse 87, Sureśvara explained the meaning of the word *na* in *na dvividhatvāt* of BUB (p. 23). Now follows the explanation of *vidyamānasya prāg anupalabdhinimittaṁ dvividhatvāt.*]

Since what covers[1] effect (a thing) is of two types, one does not see the effect which is covered by that (viz. the covering).[2] (The two-fold covering is thus explained: (i) Thatched wall etc. (is the cover) for what has come into existence[3] and (ii) (there is) covering (of the effect) by the (material) cause before the production.[4] [88]

This explains why an (earlier) existent effect is not perceived (*anupalabdha*) before it is (said to be) produced.

[1]This means 'It keeps the cause and the effect obscure'.

[2]There is a variant *nekṣyate*, whose translation could be 'an effect is not perceived covered as it is by that (covering).' It is possible that this variant could be the correct word intended by Sureśvara—cf. *kimarthaṁ nopalabhyate* in verse 90 below. However, both the AnSS edition and the NKL edition ignore this variant.

[3]A pot, for instance, or anything within a hamlet.
[4]That remains unseen and therefore *anupalabdha*.

मृदात्मनोपसंश्लिष्टं कार्यं कारणतामितम् ॥
कारणत्वाद्धि तत्स्थं तत्तदृते कारणं कथम् ॥ ८९ ॥

(Indeed) an effect (viz. a pot) which is covered by clay was (at that time) in the state of the cause[1]. Because (clay) is its cause, that (viz. the pot) is abiding in it (viz. clay[2]). How indeed could (clay) be the cause without that (viz. the effect) (that was not in existence)?[3] [89]

[1]In normal life one notices a wall etc. as covering a pot etc. That means: The two exist apart from each other.

[2]Before the production of the pot, it does not have any shape and also the name pot. It remains in the form of clay—this is its being covered by the latter.

[3]Unless there was clay etc. (i.e. cause), the pot etc. (i.e. the effect) could not be produced.

यदि कारणसंस्थं सत्तन्निमित्तं च कारणम् ॥
व्यवधानान्तराभावात्किमर्थं नोपलभ्यते ॥ ९० ॥

One might ask: If (an effect) is existent in (the state of) the cause and the cause is for (the manifestation of) the thing, then, in the absence of any other covering, why is it that it (viz. the effect) is not perceived[1]? [90]

This means 'both the cause and the effect, being ever existent, the effect should be noticeable (*sadopalabdha*)'.

[1]Cf. note 2 under verse 88 above.

कार्यान्तरेण संस्थानान्मृदादेर्नोपलभ्यते ॥
सदात्मनोपलब्धिस्तु न कदाचन हीयते ॥ ९१ ॥

[Now Sureśvara introduces the thought regarding *abhibyakti* 'manifestation' and *tirobhūti* 'concealment' of an effect.]

(A pot etc.) is not perceived since other effects (of clay etc.) are in existence, but the perception (of the effect) as of the nature of an existent is never wanting (lit. lost). [91]

The basis for this verse is a doubt as to whether a pot etc. has some other particular form at the time of its existence prior to its production. The answer is: A pot etc. existed only as clay etc., even though this latter took the shape of a lump etc. before it finally took the shape of a pot etc.

नष्टोत्पन्नसदभावशब्दप्रत्ययभेदधीः ॥
अभिव्यक्तितिरोभूतिद्वैविध्यापेक्षयैव तु ॥ ९२ ॥

The various knowledge (about an effect, e.g. a pot) arises from the meanings of words, 'destroyed, produced, extant and (its) absence owing to its dependence on two-fold state, viz. manifestation (of the form) and the concealment (of the same, or of some of its parts). [92]

The linguistic usages do not cause the destruction etc. of an effect; they indicate the states in which the ever-existent effect has become perceptible.

कुड्याद्यावरणं दृष्टं भिन्नदेशं सदावृतात् ॥
कुम्भाद्यभिन्नदेशस्थं पिण्डाद्यावरणं कथम् ॥ ९३ ॥

(An objection is raised:) A covering such as wall etc. is ever seen to be abiding in a region different from that of what is covered.[1] Therefore, how can the cover, viz. lump etc. be said to exist in the same region as that of a pot etc.? [93]

[1]The idea is: We notice that a thatched wall, which can cover (i.e. conceal) a pot, can exist in a place where there is no pot etc.—that is to say: The thatched wall and the pot are perceived to be in two different places. So, what covers (*tirodhāyaka*) and what is covered (*tirohita*) should be perceived in different places.

नैवं पयोघृतादीनामेकदेशत्वदर्शनात् ॥ ९४ ॥

अनावरणता चेत्स्यात्कपालादेर्घटात्मनि ॥
अन्तर्भावान्न साध्वेतद्विभक्तानां भवेद्यतः ॥ ९५ ॥

आवृतत्वमथ मतं भङ्ग एव प्रसज्यते ॥
यत्नो न तु घटोत्पत्तौ नैवमप्युपपद्यते ॥ ९६ ॥

न हि लोकेऽस्ति नियमो घटाभिव्यक्तिहेतुकः ॥
अनेकसाधना यस्मादभिव्यक्तिरिहेक्ष्यते ॥ ९७ ॥

(In verses 94-97, Sureśvara discusses whether what covers and what is covered abide in the same place (*samānadeśatva*) or whether they are related to only one (common) cause (*eka-kāraṇatva*). Verse 93 sets aside *samānadeśatva* and verse 95 refers to *ekaśrayatva.*)

(The answer is:) This is not so, for we notice (different forms such as) milk, ghee etc. (of an existent) as abiding in just one region[1]. [94]

If (one were to say that) a potsherd etc., that rests in (clay which is) the material cause[2] of the pot, does not have any covering (for the pot); then (we say;) it would not be proper (to say so), for there could be (in a potsherd etc.), the character of a cover[3] (for the pot) only when they are different[4], (from the pot etc.). [95]

If it is held that (what they call an effort (for producing a pot) is really an effort for destroying its covering (viz. potsherds) and not for the production of the pot; that also does not stand to reason, because there is not in this world [96]

only one particular rule[5] with regard to the manifestation of the pot; and indeed that manifestation is noticed to result from many means (of production).[6] [97]

The idea is: According to the objector's view, *mṛd* 'clay' first undergoes a change and becomes *kapālas* 'potsherds' and these later on go to make a pot. Thus both the potsherds and the pot have but one material cause, i.e. they are *ekāśraya*. This objection is answered on two counts: (i) The potsherds are considered as the cause of the pot, while they persist only in that the clay that has formed the pot (and not any (other) clay)—that is, the objector's view suffers a defect called *siddhasādhanatā*. (ii) While the pot is yet to be produced, the potsherds are also not there and, therefore, it could be easily understood that they cannot cover the pot—this is the fault called *hetvasiddhi*.

[1]Milk and water (better, however, 'curds') are, contrary to the example cited by the objector, seen to obtain in but one place. The two have a capacity to cover each other (*parasparāvaraka*).

[2]*ghaṭātmani = ghṭāvasthamṛnmātravṛttitva.*

[3]Translation follows NKL reading *āvṛtitvam* for BUBV reading *āvṛtatvam* (in verse 96), for the author intends to convey the sense of *āvaraṇatva*.

[4]*vibhakta = bhinna = ghaṭasya kapālādeś ca svāśrayamṛdavavabhinnatā.*

[5]This is stated in the next verse.

[6]SP notes the variant which is not noted by the editors of both the AnSS edition and the NKL edition; viz. *ghaṭābhivyaktihetutaḥ* which means: 'Since there are more than one cause for the manifestation of the pot.'

āvaraṇabhaṅga alone is not *sufficient for the production of a pot. This is clarified in the following verses.*

दीपेनान्यो मथा चान्यस्तथा चक्रादिना परः ॥
अभिव्यक्ति प्रयात्यर्थः पुरा सन्नेव सर्वदा ॥ ९८ ॥

Indeed some object becomes manifest by a lamp, some other (viz. butter) by the churning rod and yet another (viz. a plate made of clay) by a wheel etc., (each of these) being ever in existence before.[1] [98]

This refers to the removal of what obscured the perception of the so-called effect, not to its production.

[1]This is to stress that, despite the different types of mani-

festations (mentioned here), there is but one single fact noticeable: *pūrvaṁ sann evārtho vyajyate/na tatsattve bhedaḥ* (SP).

तमोविनाशनायैव प्रदीपोऽपीति चेन्मतम् ॥
नष्टे तमसि कुम्भोऽपि स्वयमेवोपलभ्यते ॥ ९९ ॥

If it is held that a lamp etc. are (used) only for the destruction (i.e. removal) of darkness, then even a pot etc.[1] would of itself be perceived (i.e. revealed) when darkness (etc.) is removed. [99]

This verse refers to a possible objection by someone. He implies that the lamp etc. merely destroys darkness etc. and it does not make the pot etc. manifest; this implication is specifically brought out in the next verse.

[1]The word *api* after *pradīpa* in the verse indicates to the other *sādhanas*, viz. *manthana-daṇḍa* and *cakra* which are mentioned in the preceding verse. So also, *api* after *kumbha* refers to *navanīta* and *tamaḥ* indicated in that verse.

किमेवं भवतः सिद्धं यदि नाम तमोहृतिः ॥
सदेव व्यज्यते सर्वमिति नैवापनुद्यते ॥ १०० ॥

What indeed do you have established, if it is held that there is (merely) removal of darkness (etc.)? (Indeed the rule, viz.) all that is ever existent before becomes revealed, cannot be set aside. [100]

This verse answers the implication of the objector of the previous verse. It points to that the objector has unwittingly accepted Satkāryavāda.

अज्ञातत्वापमार्ष्ट्यर्थमुपादित्सन्ति मानिनः ॥
मानानि मानसंबन्धादज्ञातत्वं च नश्यति ॥ १०१ ॥

Those who have (i.e. employ) the means of knowing wish to take up (i.e. employ) the means for wiping away (i.e. removal of) the unknownness (of the object that is unknown.) (Only) when there is a connection (of any object of knowledge) with a means of knowing, the unknownness (of that object) is removed (lit. destroyed). [101]

The preceding four verses called for explanation of the function of manifestation of some object which is different from its actual production.

यतः सति क्रियाभेदे किं पूर्वमिति चोदना ॥
क्रियाभेदे न च न्याय्यं ध्वान्तनाशः क्रियाफलम् ॥ १०२ ॥

ज्ञातुर्ज्ञानाभिनिष्पत्तिर्निष्पन्नं मेयमेति सत् ॥
मेयाभिसंगतं तच्च मेयाभत्वं प्रपद्यते ॥ १०३ ॥

[These verses explain that it is not proper to raise the question of *paurvāparya* in respect of the manifestation of an object vis-a-vis its production. There is behind this discussion the following implied doubt that can be raised by someone: The previous verse refers to the connection of a means of knowledge with an object of knowing and also to the removal of ignorance in respect of that object. Which is earlier, knowledge of the object (e.g. a pot) or the removal of ignorance in respect of it?]

For, the question 'what is prior?' is raised (only) where there are different actions, and it is not proper (to ask that question) where there is non-difference in respect of them. (Now, in respect of the illustration of the lamp etc.), the removal of darkness is the result of the action. [102]

First, there is on the part of a knower the rise of the knowledge (that there is an object)[1] then it[2] touches (lit. goes to) the object of knowledge[3] and then, coming into contact with the object, it assumes the form of the object.[4] [103]

It is only clear that only after the removal of ignorance (in respect of a lamp etc.) there occurs the knowledge of it (on the part of one.) This is clarified in the next verse.

[1]This is *viṣayābhāsa* 'appearance of (an earlier existing) object.'

[2]Translation follows the reading *tat* of BVS for *sat* in BUBV and NKL.

[3]The appearance of the object to one.

[4]This refers to *viṣayākāratā* of the intellect of the knower. This is to say: Intellect (*Buddhi*) grasps the appearances of an object before the knower and assumes its shape. Thus, it removes the cover on the object (i.e. manifests it) that is *ajñānahāni*. This is to say: *ajñānahāni* and *ghaṭajñāna* are not two actions or happenings—and that explains the significance of *kriyābheda* = *kriyā-abheda* in verse 102. All these make up a knowledge-situation. Cf. *jñānasya utpatti-viṣayasambandha-viṣayākārabhajana-ajñānahānānāṁ kramaḥ suprasiddha ity arthaḥ* (NKL).

व्यवधानं तमो यस्माद्धटोऽयमिति संविदः ॥
प्रकाशवद्धटं चर्ते कुतस्तत्तमसो ह्नुतिः ॥ १०४ ॥

Since darkness[1] is an obstacle to (i.e. the curtain over) the knowledge 'this is a pot', (there is no knowledge of it).[2] Whence can there be concealment (i.e. removal) of darkness, if there does not exist a pot which is pervaded by light?[3] [104]

[1]This means 'ignorance'.

[2]This is implied. Only then, the meaning of the first line becomes clear.

[3]There is need of light which manifests a pot. Thus, it is a means of kowing the pot. Knowledge of the pot is the result and that is equivalent to the removal of the ignorance about it—this was pointed out by *kriyāphalam* in verse 102 and is clarified in verse 105.

प्रमाणव्यापृतेर्ज्ञातोऽज्ञातोऽज्ञातत्वहानिकृत् ॥
घटोऽवगत इत्येतत्ततः संपद्यते फलम् ॥ १०५ ॥

A pot which was formerly unknown now becomes known thanks to the operation of the means of knowing and therefore becomes the destroyer of its own unknownness. Thereafter follows this result, viz. (the awareness that) this pot is (now) known.[1]

[1]SP reads *tataś cādānādivyavahārasiddhiḥ*. Further, NKL makes a note-worthy observation: *ato vyañjakasya nāvaraṇabhaṅga eva yatnaḥ*—this refers to verses 96 and 97 above.

यद्यावरणभङ्गाय यत्नः स्याद्घटवित्तये ॥
कार्यान्तरं भवेद्भङ्गात्तेनाप्यावृतता घटे ॥ १०६ ॥

[Here follows further discussion of *āvaraṇabhaṅga*.]

(This is an objection:) The effort for destroying the cover (on a pot) were to be made (only) for knowing the pot, then there would arise another result (or effect[1]) from the destruction (of the cover) and thereby also would there be the state of being covered (in respect of that) pot (yet further). [106]

[1]This refers to the powdered clay of the lump etc. (*vidala-cūrṇādi*). And that would still cause the concealment of the pot.

व्यवधानान्तरं तस्मादन्यदप्यापतेत्तदा ॥
अतो नियत एवात्र व्यापारः फलवान्भवेत् ॥ १०७ ॥

Then there would follow from that yet another obstacle (to the perception of the pot) and therefore only a specific activity (of the means of knowing) would have here[1] the (desired) result. [107]

If one still persisted to hold *āvaraṇabhaṅga* in respect of *vidala-cūrṇādi*, there would follow further obstacles in the form of yet other effects in *infinite regress*. NKL adds: *tasmād arthavyaktyartho vyañjakavyāpāro 'rthavān*.

[1]This means 'knowing a pot'.

अतीतैष्यद्घटज्ञानं सद्घटालम्बनं भवेत् ॥
घटज्ञानत्वतः साक्षादिहत्यघटबोधवत् ॥ १०८ ॥

अतीतोऽनागतोऽर्थोऽसन्यदि वाभ्युपगम्यते ॥
अतीतानागतज्ञानं मिथ्येशस्य प्रसज्यते ॥ १०९ ॥

प्रत्यक्षं नापि चेशस्य केनचित्प्रतिहन्यते ॥
अपविद्धातिशीत्येव तज्ज्ञानं केन हन्यते ॥ ११० ॥

घटसत्त्वे पुरोत्पत्तेरनुमा च प्रदर्शिता ॥
तस्मात्सदेव कार्यं स्यात्प्रागुत्पत्तेरपि ध्रुवम् ॥ १११ ॥

[Verses 108-111 explain another reason for holding all-time existence of the effect. They explain *atītānāgatapratyayabhedāc ca* (BUB p. 25). Before verse 108, Sureśvara has refuted the arguments regarding (i) non-perception of a pot which had not been produced, and (ii) inference related to the non-manifest pot. But, since they make effort towards the production of a pot that will come into existence and also they accept the knowledge on the part of Yogins of the pots in the past and also of the future, he proceeds to discuss the same.]

The knowledge of a pot which has been existent in the past and of that which will be existent in future would be dependent on (only) an existent pot, since it is the knowledge of a pot comparable to the direct perception of a pot that exists here (in front of us). [108]

If one were to accept an object as non-existent in the past[1] and (also) in the future[2], there would follow the contingency that the knowledge of the Lord in respect of the past and of the future[2] is (or, has to be) held as false ![3] [109]

And the direct perception by the Lord (of any object) is not objected to by any one. Who then can object to His knowledge which has set aside (the possibility of) any excelling (knowledge)? [110]

And we have (already) adduced the reason for proving the existence of a pot (even) before the production (of it).

Therefore, it is certainly that an effect exists even before its production. [111]

[1]This means 'Before its production.'

[2]This means 'After it is destroyed.'

[3]The Tārkika accepts that the Lord is possessed of *atita-anāgata-jñāna* and, therefore, the knowledge of an object non-existent in the past and in the future which he has attributed to Him would have to be declared as false (*mithyā*). This should mean that the Tārkika is involving internal contradiction in his philosophy (*bhrāntatva*).

एष्यद्घटनिषेधे च विरोधोऽपि प्रसज्यते ॥
भविष्यति न भाव्यर्थो वर्तमाननिषेधवत् ॥ ११२ ॥

[Verses 112-119 are refutation of the argument of those of who posit the non-existence of an effect.]

And[1] in case one rejects (the existence of) a pot which is going to come into existence also,[2] there forcefully follows opposition; to say that a forthcoming object will not be in existence is like denying the existence of an existent pot. [112]

This argument pertains to the state of a pot at the time when one is active in producing it.

[1]This connects the argument of the verse with that in verse 109 above.

[2]This implies the existence of a pot that existed in the past.

गृह्यमाणो घटो नासन्निति यद्वद्विरुध्यते ॥
अतीतैष्यन्मितघटप्रतिषेधस्तथाविधः ॥ ११३ ॥

As a pot which is being grasped (i.e. seen) cannot be denied by (saying that) it is not existent, so also there cannot be the denial of a pot known as of the past or as one coming into existence (in future). [113]

This pertains to *atha prāg utpatter ghaṭo 'sann iti*.... (BUB p. 26).

This first line of the verse has to be construed thus: *yadvad gṛhyamāṇo ghaṭo asann iti na virudhyate*. SP notes *no 'sanniti* as a variant for *nāsann iti*; this is confirmed by the edition of NKL.

प्रागभावादयोऽभावाः सन्तः स्युरतिरेकिणः ॥
व्यपदेशाद्घटेनैषामन्योन्याभाववद्ध्रुवम् ॥ ११४ ॥

(One might object:) The non-existences, viz. prior non-existence etc.[1], which are existents distinct[2] (from a pot etc.) would certainly be existents on account of their mention apart from that of a pot (etc.) just as in the case of mutually exclusive objects.[3] [114]

The argument is based on two considerations: (i) *prāgabhāva* etc. are mentioned as distinct *padārthas*, and (ii) the notion of *anyonyābhāva* can be entertained (only) if there are two distinct *padārthas*.

[1]There are in addition: *dhvaṁsābhāva*, *atyantābhāva* and *anyonyābhāva*.

[2]The word *atirekiṇaḥ* literally means 'having an existence apart from or over and above (a pot).'

[3]The idea is: As *ghaṭe paṭo nāsti* and *paṭe ghaṭo nāsti* point to two mutually exclusive existents, so also would *ghaṭe prāgabhāvo nāsti* and *prāgabhāve ghaṭo nāsti* show the two as distinct existents.

एवं च सति संबन्धो न भावाभावयोर्मिथः ॥
विरोधाद्भावयोर्यद्वदेकत्वान्नाप्यभावयोः ॥ ११५ ॥

[This is the answer to the objection above.]

In case this is so, there would be no mutual connection between an existent and its (previous) non-existence owing to their mutual opposition. (So) also, there cannot be any connection between two non-existences like that between two existents since these two are of but one nature. [115]

The idea is : When there is *prāgabhāva* (or any other *abhāva*) of a pot, there is no *bhāva* 'existence' of it and, consequently, any connection between them (e.g. *anyonyābhāva* of them) cannot be established.

असतश्च न संबन्धोऽकारकत्वात्कथंचन ॥
संबन्धश्च क्रियात्मत्वान्न सिध्येत्कारकं विना ॥ ११६ ॥

Further, what is non-existent does not have any connection whatever (with an existent), because it (viz. the connection) does not have a cause[1] for producing it. And since (bringing about) a connection has the nature of an action, it would not be brought about in the absence of any agent.[2] [116]

This is yet another argument as to why the non-existence cannot get connected with an existent.

[1]*akārakatva* = *akāraṇatva*.

[2]*kāraka* = *kartṛ*. The idea is based on the explanation of *sambandha* which is either *samavāya* or *saṁyoga* and which gets established owing to some factor determining it (*kāraṇa*) or by the effort of some agent (*kartṛ*).

प्रागभावो घटस्येति घट एवोच्यते यदि ॥
घट एव घटस्येति व्यपदेशो न युज्यते ॥ ११७ ॥

If (one might argue:) By saying 'there is previous non-existence[1] of a pot, we refer only to that pot itself, then (our reply is:) In that case, the mention (which is tantamount to saying) 'there is a pot of a pot' would not stand to reason. [117]

[1]Previous non-existence is indicative of other *abhāvas* of the pot.

न चासत्त्वं घटस्यैवं प्रागभावो घटो न च ॥
अवध्यवधिमद्भेदे प्रागभावोऽपि सिध्यति ॥ ११८ ॥

And this cannot prove the (previous) non-existence of a pot; so also is not the prior non-existence of the pot the pot (itself), for when distinction is accepted (between a limitor[1] and the limited (viz. the pot) the prior non-existence (of the pot, for instance,) also gets established. [118]

[1]NKL: *avadhiḥ pratiyogi, tadvān abhāvaḥ*. This points to a pot and its prior absence.

अथ प्रकल्प्य संबन्धं घटस्येत्यभिधीयते ॥
क्लृप्तस्यैव ह्यभावस्य व्यपदेशः प्रसज्यते ॥ ११९ ॥

Now, having imagined the relation of the prior non-existence (of a pot) and the pot, (one says) that there is prior non-existence of the pot, then it will be contingent that there is the name (pot) for even (this) imaginary non-existence. [119]

The argument in this verse is based on an imaginary connection between previous non-existence (of a pot) and the pot and which is similar to the imaginary connection between an individual (body) and sentience. SP significantly points to such a connection as is understood in the phrase 'Rāhu's head,' which, in reality, does not belong to a full intact body.

अर्थान्तरमभावश्चेदुक्तं संस्मर्तुमर्हसि ॥
शशशृङ्गादिकल्पस्य घटस्य स न युज्यते ॥ १२० ॥

स्वहेतुसत्तासंबन्धः संबन्धस्य सदाश्रयात् ॥

(If it is said:) non-existence is (altogether) a different object, then you (i.e. who say this) should remember our argument made earlier,[1] viz. that (connection) of the pot which is (imaginary) like the horns of a hare, [120]

with the existence of its own cause is not logically understood, since (such) connection rests (always) on what are existent objects. [121[ab]]

[1]This is verse 11 above : *vyatireke sad evāsat*. One cannot say that one of the two connected things is real and the other, unreal, for, in so saying, one makes a positive mistake.

अथास्त्वयुतसिद्धानां नासतोऽयुतसिद्धता ॥ १२१ ॥

[Verses 121^{cd}-122 are a discussion of the Tārkika's notion of *janma* of an object which was non-existent before. It consists in either *sattāsamavāya* or *svakāraṇasamavāya*.]

Now if (someone were to say:) let that connection obtain between things which are inseparably associated, (our answer is:) There is no inseparable association of a non-existent (with an existent). [121^{cd}]

न भावाभावयोर्योगो नापि चायमभावयोः ॥
सतोरेव यतो योगः सिद्धं कार्यमतः सदा ॥ १२२ ॥

[This explains *asmāt sad eva kāryaṁ prāg utpatteḥ* (BUB p. 29).]

There is no connection between existence and non-existence; not also is there a connection between two non-existences, since there is a connection only between two existent things; therefore, the effect is ever an established entity. [122]

द्वैतैकत्वात्मकं रूपं वैराजं कार्यमात्मनः ॥
समुद्र एव ह्यस्येति विराट्कारणमब्रवीत् ॥ १२३ ॥

[Verses 123-124 explain the meaning of the word *mṛtyu* in *mṛtyunaivedam āvṛtam āsīt* (BUB 1.2.1).]

The form which is of the nature of oneness in duality is (the form of) Virāj and (also) an effect of the Ātman; (the Śruti[1]) has declared Virāj as the cause of this (world) in the words 'just the Samudra...' [123]

[1]SP points to *agnir mūrdhā* . . as the Śruti passage and shows that it is followed by the Smṛti : *apa eva sasarjādau* . . (*Manusmṛti* 1.8^{cd})

संभूय कार्यभूतानि भूतयोनिं यतो विभुम् ॥
जन्मस्थितिलयान्यान्ति समुद्रस्तेन विश्वकृत् ॥ १२४ ॥

Since all the beings which have been effects, having attained their birth, sustenance and destruction in the all pervading source of the elements, merge (in it)[1], therefore, Samudra is called the maker of all (that exists). [124]

[1]Cf. *janmādy asya yataḥ* (BS 1.1.2) and BSB on it.

Verses 125-148 *explain how the notion about the Lord as the creator etc. of the world is but a product of Nescience.*

तत्समुद्रं परं ब्रह्म संविन्मात्रसतत्त्वकम् ॥
अविज्ञातात्मयाथात्म्यं हेतुत्वेनेह शब्द्यते ॥ १२५ ॥

That highest Brahman, Samudra[1], which is merely of the nature of Sentience, and whose real nature has not been known, is mentioned here[2] as the cause (of the world). [125]

[1]The use of the word *samudra* in the neuter is to be noted—that refers to the Brahman.

[2]In the sentence *mṛtyuneva*... (BU 1.2.1).

इदं जगदुपादानं सर्वशक्त्यजमव्ययम् ॥
स्वात्मैकाज्ञानवृत्तेन ग्रसिष्णु प्रभविष्णु च ॥ १२६ ॥

This, one who has this universe for the material cause (of its creation), who is omnipotent, unborn and imperishable, is, on account of the effect of its own ignorance[1] of itself, the devourer and the ruler (of this world).[2] [126]

[1]This is to strengthen the notion of *avijñātātmayāthātmya* in the previous verse—the power of Nescience.

[2]Refer to the unborn Prakṛti which is the same as *avidyā*; see *Śvetāśvataropaniṣad* 4.5[ab]: *ajām ekāṁ lohitaśuklakṛṣṇāṁ bahviḥ prajāḥ sṛjamānāṁ sarūpāḥ*; *Sāṁkhyakārikā* 1[ab]: *ajām ekāṁ lohitaśuklakṛṣṇāṁ bahviḥ prajāḥ sṛjamānāṁ namāmaḥ*. However, the Brahman is not, like Prakṛti, to modify itself in reality. It appears that it has modified itself. The verse refutes a notion of those who would compare the modification of the Brahman to the modification of milk into curds.

स्वाभासवर्त्मनैवैतत्स्वात्माज्ञानजभूमिषु ॥
इतं बहुत्वमेकं सद्वियद्यद्वद्घटादिषु ॥ १२७ ॥

This unique existent has assumed multiplicity (i.e. multiple forms) in the different forms[1] (which are) produced from Ignorance of its own nature, through (its own) appearances[2]—(this happens) in the same way as the sky (appears) in (the form of) a pot etc. [127]

[1]These are Hiraṇyagarbha, Virāj etc.

[2]This emphasises the unreal character of the worldly objects, or rather the notion that the variety of the world arises out of Nescience.

अकारणं सदज्ञानात्कारणत्वं यथैत्यजम् ॥
सर्वकारकतामेवं क्रियातत्फलतामपि ॥ १२८ ॥

As the existent which is not (in reality) a cause[1] becomes the cause[2] on account of Ignorance,[3] in the same way it attains the character of the maker of all and the nature of all activity and its results. [128]

Here SP refers to the Śruti passages which seem to show that the Brahman is the cause.

[1]The word *akāraṇa* can be alternatively translated as 'not having a cause (for its own existence),' but we prefer the translation above since the verse goes further to mention it thus:

kāraṇatvam and *sarvakāraṇatām ejati*. See also *tad etad brahmāpūrvam anaparam...* (BU 2.5.19).

[2]That is the origin of the world.

[3]This is the brief expression of the contents of the preceding verse.

साध्यसाधनतां तस्मादज्ञानैकव्यपाश्रयाम् ॥
उच्चैरनूद्य तत्तत्त्वं वेदान्ताः प्रत्यपीपदन् ॥ १२६ ॥

Therefore, having clearly (lit. loudly) declared time and again[1] the nature (of the Brahman) as the cause of the effects[2] which rests solely on ignorance (about the true nature of the Ātman), the Vedāntas have established the true nature of the same (i.e. the Brahman). [129]

This verse intends to point out the true significance of the Śruti passages which refer to the creation of the world by the Brahman (*sṛṣṭyādiśrutivākyāni*).

[1]This is the force of *anu* in *anūdya*.

[2]This means 'the world full of variety'.

अकारणमकार्यं सत्कार्यकारणतामगात् ॥
मोहादेव ततः शास्त्रं तदुच्छित्तौ प्रवर्तते ॥ १३० ॥

The existent which is neither a cause[1] nor an effect has attained the nature of a cause of an effect owing only to ignorance (lit. delusion); therefore, the (Upaniṣadic) lore proceeds to destroy that.[2] [130]

[1]Cf. note 1 (on *akāraṇa*) in verse 128 above. This is supported by NKL which points to *Taittirīyopaniṣad* 2.6: *sac ca tyac cābhavat* and adds *iti sattārthabhavatiprayogāt pāramārthikam eva kāraṇatvam atrāha*.

[2]Read: *asyānarthahetoḥ prahāṇāya* (*ātmaikatvavidyāpratipattaye*) *sarve vedāntā ārabhyante* (BSB p. 45).

अपीताशेषसंसारं शुद्धसंस्कारसंश्रयम् ॥
अव्याकृतमिदं ब्रह्म ह्यन्तर्यामीति चोच्यते ॥ १३१ ॥

And this (very) Brahman which has withdrawn (lit. swallowed[1]) the entire universe, which alone[2] affords support for (various) modifications,[3] (and) which has not differentiated itself, is called the entrant within.[4] [131]

[1]BUBV reads *apitāśeṣasaṁsāraṁ* but NKL edition reads *āpitāśeṣasaṁsāraṁ*. The latter is possibly simplifying the text. Whatever be the reading, meaning remains the same.

[2]The word *śuddham* means *kevalam*, i.e. all by itself.

[3]SP rightly observes: *saṁśrayaśabdo bhāvapradhānaḥ saṁskārasya saṁśrayaḥ saṁśrayaṇam svasminn iti vā saṁsāradaśāto viśeṣam āha.*

[4]That which resides in every individual—the individual self. It is affected by the limiting adjuncts.

अज्ञानानुपमर्देन व्याकृतिर्यास्य जायते ॥
स्वप्नविज्ञानवन्नासौ सत्यमयव्यपाश्रया ॥ १३२ ॥

सम्यग्ज्ञानसमुत्पत्तौ हेतुत्वं तु निगच्छति ॥
निद्रां हत्वा यतः स्वप्नज्ञानादपि विबुध्यते ॥ १३३ ॥

Whatever modification[1] of this (world) is produced on account of the non-removal (lit. non-destruction) of ignorance has no basis in the true (existent) object of knowing[2] in the same way as the knowledge obtained (by one) in one's dream has no basis (in true objects).[3] [132]

But it[4] becomes[5] the cause for the rise of the correct knowledge (of the true nature of the Brahman), since one is brought to reality (lit. is awakened) from the knowledge acquired in the dream after it has removed (lit. destroyed) one's sleep. [133]

[1]It means appearance of the world.

[2]That is, the Brahman.

[3]This argument is similar to that in the *vaitathyaprakaraṇa* of the *Gauḍpādakārikā*.

[4]SP refers it to some Śruti which might be false and can yet

become the cause for one's becoming aware of the true nature of the Brahman. This is like the argument in BSB (pp. 40 ff.) where Śruti, a false *pramāṇaprameyavyavahāra* is discussed as a means for removing ignorance.

It appears, nevertheless, that it here refers to *vyākṛti* mentioned just in the preceding verse and can include the *pramāṇaprameya-vyavahāra*. It is not necessary, therefore, to follow SP.

[5]In *nigacchati*, the preposition *ni* causes no change in the sense of the root *gam*.

उपेयप्रतिपत्त्यैव प्रमाणानां प्रमाणता ॥
वस्तुस्थित्या न सत्यत्वमिति पूर्वमवादिषम् ॥ १३४ ॥

The means of knowing can really serve as the means of knowing by bringing about (the knowledge of) what is sought to be known (lit. approached). And I have said earlier that there is not (in these means) validity, owing to factual state of reality.[1] [134]

Cf. verses 126-128 and 132 above.

नामरूपादिना येयमविद्या प्रथतेऽसती ॥
माया तस्याः परं सौक्ष्म्यं मृत्युनैवेति भण्यते ॥ १३५ ॥

[Now follows the meaning of the word *mṛtyu*.]

The most minuteness of this one[1], viz. what is called Ignorance, and what (though) non-extant, amplifies itself by (bearing various) names, forms etc.[2] is (and is also called) Māyā[3], is mentioned (here in the BU) by the word Mṛtyu.[4] [135]

[1]This refers to the commonly known ignorance also, not merely the one that is inferred from the apparent effects (as discussed in the preceding verses).

[2]The word 'etc.' stands for *karman*.

[3]The author has brought in *māyā* for showing that *avidyā* and *māyā* are but one.

[4]SP explains this as *avyaktanāmarūpa*, *adhyakṣādyayogya* and *apañcikṛtamahābhūtāvasthātirikta* and *māyārūpa*.

मृत्युर्वै तम इत्येवमाप एवेदमित्यपि ॥
अविद्या प्रथते मौली व्यक्ताव्यक्तात्मनानिशम् ॥ १३६ ॥

In the sentence 'Mṛtyu is indeed darkness'[1] and also in the sentence 'Waters themselves are this universe'[2], there ever reveals the basic Ignorance[3] in its form of the manifest and the non-manifest. [136]

[1]*Taittirīya Brāhmaṇa* 1.4.7.5 and 7—this refers to an individual's natural (i.e. common) knowledge and activity.

[2]BU 5.5.1 ; this refers to it as the origin (*kāraṇa*) of waters.

[3]Here Sureśvara intends to convey that the two sentences refer only to *mūlāvidyā*.

एतेभ्योऽसौ समुत्थाय स्वाभासानात्मजन्मना ॥
याति क्षेत्रज्ञतामीशः कूटस्थोऽपि ह्यविद्यया ॥ १३७ ॥

[This verse shows how the Lord Himself appears as an individual self.]

Indeed, having arisen from these (known five) elements, i.e. through the rise of the modifications, that Lord[1], though immutable, becomes the knower of a field[2]—(this is) on account of Ignorance. [137]

[1]The word *asau* refers to the one called Mṛtyu, the Lord.

[2]A field is a body and the knower of a field is an individual self.

आपो ह्यणुतराः सत्यमसृजन्तेति हि श्रुतिः ॥
क्रियाविज्ञानशक्त्यात्मा सोऽपि ब्रह्मासृजत्परः ॥ १३८ ॥

Indeed the Śruti (has declared:) 'More minute (i.e. subtle) waters[1] created Truth[2]. And that highest Lord, who was (possessed) of the nature of knowledge for activity, created the Brahman. [138]

This verse refers to a *sṛṣṭivākya* in the Śruti which proves that the origin of the world is in fact the unmanifest and not Hiraṇyagarbha (or Mṛtyu) who is said to be overpowered by desire for food etc.

[1]Read BU 5.5.1 : *satyam brahma* and BUB on it : *satyam brahma prathamajam, tad etad dhiraṇyagarbhasya sūtrātmano janma*—this refers to the most minute state of the waters, viz. *apañcīkṛtapañcabhūtātmakasūtra.*

[2]This refers to the *apañcīkṛta* state of them.

विराड्ब्रह्माथ ससृजे मनुं देवं प्रजापतिम् ॥
मनुर्देवान्मनुष्यांश्च स्थास्नु कृत्स्नं चरिष्णु च ॥ १३९ ॥

Then Virāj, the Brahman, created[1] Manu, the divine Prajāpati ('Lord of subjects') and Manu created Gods and human beings, the entire non-moving (lit. standing) and moving world (of objects). [139]

[1]The word *sasṛje* is Vedic Ātmanepada for Parasmaipada. Possibly the Vedic passive sense is purposely conveyed by Sureśvara—that is to say; this creation is to be understood as appearance of creation.

साध्यसाधनवत्कृत्स्नकार्यरूपविवक्षया ॥
श्रुतिः प्रववृते सेयं नैवेहेतीह यत्नतः ॥ १४० ॥

This well-known (*sā*) Śruti passage, beginning with the words *naiveha* has commenced (to convey its contents) with the desire to declare specifically (the manifestation of) all the effects (comprising of) what is to be produced and what are the means of producing the same. [140]

NKL points out that Sureśvara intends to refer to BU 1.2.1—1.4.7.

अशनायापिपासाभ्यां मृत्यो रूपं प्रचक्षते ॥
प्राणस्य तत्र संवर्गाद्वागाद्यध्यात्मदैवयोः ॥ १४१ ॥

By the words *aśanāyā* and *pipāsā*, they declare the nature of Mṛtyu. (that is) Prāṇa, owing to the absorption[1] into Prāṇa[2] of the different parts of the body such as speech etc.[3] and of the deities superintending over them. [141]

[1]The word *saṁvarga* refers to 'absorption'; cf. the story of Raikva in *Chāndogyopaniṣad* 4.3.1-3 (4.3.1 on *adhyātman* and 4.3.3 on *adhidaiva*).

[2]Prāṇa conveys two senses: (i) the Ātman and (ii) the wind.

[3]*vāgādadhyātma-* of AnSS edition is to be corrected *vāgādya-dhyātma-*

The word *adhyātmadaiva* is a peculiar compound; *adhi* is to be compounded with each *ātman* and *daiva*.

एतस्माज्जायते प्राणो मनः सर्वेन्द्रियाणि च ॥
खं वायुर्ज्योतिरापश्च पृथ्वी विश्वस्य धारिणी ॥ १४२ ॥

सृष्टिमेतां समुद्दिश्य तन्मनोऽकुरुतेति या ॥
श्रुतिः प्रवृत्ता निर्वक्तुं यावदव्याकृतं परा ॥ १४३ ॥

"From this one is born Prāṇa, *manas* and all sense-organs, sky, wind, fire, water, and further, the earth which is the supporter of all."[1] [142]

Keeping in view (the purport of) this (account of) creation (in the Śruti just quoted), the other Śruti (viz. BU 1.2.1) has proceeded to explain the same in (the passage beginning with the statement: *tan mano akuruta* etc. up to the later statement) this (world) was (then) not manifest (viz. BU 1.4.7). [143]

[1]This is a quotation of the statement of creation in *Muṇḍakopaniṣad* 2.1.3.

यद्वा विराजमुद्दिश्य संकल्पमकरोन्मनः ॥
आत्मन्वी स्यामिति तथा साकूतः सृष्टिकारणः ॥ १४४ ॥

[This explains *tad iti manaso nirdeśaḥ* (BUB p. 29). It presents another explanation of *tan mano akuruta.*]

Or, (Hiraṇyagarbha) the cause of (this) creation, who had a thought (in mind): 'Let me be possessed of (a) self (or, a body[1]),' created *manas*, the one which collects impressions[2] in an orderly way (*sam*), having the intention of creating Virāj. [144]

[1]*ātmanvī—ātmavān—aham anenātmanā manasā manasvī syām ity abhiprāyaḥ* (BUB p. 29); this should signify the sense 'possessed of a body'.

[2]The word *saṁkalpa* is used in apposition to *manas*; it means *saṁkalpaka*.

स्वविभूतीक्षणं सृष्टौ विभोरर्चनमुच्यते ।
आपोऽजायन्त इति च सर्वभूतोपलक्षणम् ॥ १४५ ॥

[Now follows the explanation of *so 'rcan* (BUB 1.2.1).]

(This) thinking[1] about his own manifold form (lit. expansion) (on the part) of the (all-)pervader, in respect of the (proposed) creation, is called, (his) Arcana (worship). And (the Śruti sentence) *āpo 'jāyanta*[2] is indicative of all elements[3] (to be created later). [145]

[1]The root *ikṣ* means 'to think'; cf. *ikṣater nāśabdam* (BS 1.1.5). But read BUB (p. 30): *arcann arcayan pūjayan...arcataḥ pūjayataḥ* (*āpo rasātmikāḥ pūjāṅgabhūtā ajāyantotpannāḥ*) ! Also, cf. the derivation of the name Arka in verse 147 below from root *arc* 'to think'.

[2]SP holds the absence of Saṁdhi of *āpo 'jāyanta* and *iti* as an indication of Sureśvara's regard for the Śruti text. That is to say; one should not expect to have *āpo ajāyanteti* by mixing Vedic speech with the popular parlance.

[3]These are: *ākāśa*, *vāyu*, *tejas* and *pṛthivī* which were *pañcīkṛta.* But SP refers to *ākāśāditraya*, since the *Taittirīyopaniṣad* refers to *ākāśādisṛṣṭi* and Śaṅkara and Sureśvara belonged to the Taittirīya school. Read : *atrākāśaprabhṛtīnāṁ trayāṇām utpattyanantaram iti*

vaktavyam śrutyantarasāmarthyād vikalpāsambhavāc ca (BUB p. 30). That means : *āpaḥ* is not intended.

विद्योत्पत्तिप्रधानत्वात्सृष्टिर्वा न विवक्ष्यते ॥
तथा च प्रतिवेदान्तं सृष्टिर्नानाविधेक्ष्यते ॥ १४६ ॥

[This is Sureśvara's comment on BUB p. 30 quoted above. Therefore, NKL's remark: *vārtikatvasiddhyartham vidyeti.* It is to be understood, therefore, the verse 146 is a Vārtika in the sense of *duruktacintā.*]

Or (perhaps) (making any statement about) creation is not intended, owing to (the intent of the Vedānta on) considering the rise of knowledge as the principal (purport). So indeed in the different texts of the Vedānta is noticed various (description of) creation.[1] [146]

[1]SP points out that the account of creation in the *Taittirīyopaniṣad* begins with *ākāśa*, in the *Chāndogyopaniṣad*, with *tejas*, and in the *Muṇḍakopaniṣad* with *prāṇa*. Then it remarks that the *Aitareyopaniṣad* does not have any specific order. Probably, this fact prompted Sureśvara to offer an alternative (and, perhaps, better) explanation.

अर्चतो मे यतो जज्ञे कमम्भः सुखकृत्ततः ॥
अर्काभिधोऽथ संवृत्तः प्राणो मृत्युः प्रजापतिः ॥ १४७ ॥

Because (he thought:) 'While I am thinking (i.e. offering worship) there was produced water which brought (me) pleasure', therefore Prāṇa, Mṛtyu and Prajāpati became known by the name Arka. [147]

This is derivation of the name Arka from root *ṛc*>*arc* 'to think' (cf. *arcana* in verse 145 above) and *ka* 'water'. A peculiar derivation from a verbal root and a noun !

उपासनमतोऽस्यापि नाग्नेरेवेति निश्चितिः ॥
अर्कनामाभिसंबन्धो नोपासनमृते यतः ॥ १४८ ॥
यदि वाऽग्नेरिदं नाम तस्य प्रकरणित्वतः ॥

[The verse states the purport of this derivation.]

Therefore, the decision is that there is (prescribed) the worship of this one (i.e. Arka) also and not only of Agni, since there cannot obtain any connection of the name of Arka (with worship) without the worship (offered to him).[1] [148]

Or rather this name (viz. Arka) belongs to Agni, for he is the subject of the section.[2] [149ab]

[1]This has a reference to the Śruti: *kaṁ ha vā asmai bhavati ya evam etad arkasyārkatāṁ veda* (BU 1.2.1). This *phalaśruti* would have become meaningless if the name Arka did not mean Hiraṇyagarbha or Prāṇa or Mṛtyu.

[2]Arka as Agni could suggest itself on the basis of another derivation of that name, viz. from the root *ṛc* 'to shine'. But that does not seem to have attracted Sureśvara's attention !

आपो वा अर्क इति तु चित्यनामार्थमेव तत् ॥ १४९ ॥

[Verses 149cd-162 pertain to BU 1.2.2.]

And (the Śruti statement) *āpo vā arkaḥ* is for (conveying) the name of one which is to be collected (viz. fire)[1] (according to the dictate of the scriptures). [149cd]

Cf. verse 145 above on this verse. Yet, worth noting is BUB p. 30: *āpo vā arkaḥ/kaḥ punar asāv arka iti/ucyate/āpo vāiyā arcanāṅga-bhūtās tā evārko 'gner arkasya hetutvāt/apsu cāgniḥ pratiṣṭhita iti/na punaḥ sākṣād evārkas tāḥ/tāsām aprakaraṇāt/agneś ca prakaraṇam/vakṣyati cāyam agnir arka iti/*And yet more worth noting is that Sureśvara has left this portion of BUB unconsidered !

[1]The name here mentioned is Arka.

शर आसीदिति गिरा शक्त्यवस्था विवक्ष्यते ॥
सा पृथिव्यभवच्चेति विराजो जन्मशब्दनम् ॥ १५० ॥

In the statement of the Śruti *śara āsīt*,[1] it is intended to convey the state (of the Brahman, the Sūtrātman) having the capacity[2] (for creation). And the statement *sā pṛthivy abhavat* is the assertion of (the fact, viz.) the birth of Virāj.[3] [150]

[1]The sentence reads: *tad yad apāṁ śara āsīt.*

[2]The word *śaktyavasthā* means *śakti-mad-avasthā.*

[3]This sentence completes the meaning of *tat samahanyata* 'it became consistent'.

तपोऽप्सु तप्यमानासु ह्यण्डं जज्ञे हिरण्मयम् ॥
इति श्रुतिर्जगादार्थं यथैवेह प्रपञ्च्यते ॥ १५१ ॥

Here[1] is explained the idea of (the fact, viz.) creation as another Śruti has declared it in the words 'while the waters were performing penance...in (the waters) being heated there was born a golden egg'.[2] [151]

[1]That is; in BU 1.2.2.

[2]This is a quotation from the *Śatapatha Brāhmaṇa* which, in full, reads thus: *āpo ha vā idam agra āsuḥ/salilam eva tā akāmayanta kathaṁ nu prajāyemahīti/tā aśrāmyanstās tapo 'tapyanta, tāsu tapas tapyamānāsu tāsv antar hiraṇmayam aṇḍaṁ sambabhūva.*

एवं व्यष्टिसमष्टयात्मा वैराजं देहमात्मनः ॥
प्राचीक्लृपदथेदानीं सृष्टिस्तस्य विवक्ष्यते ॥ १५२ ॥

Thus the Brahman of the nature of individuality and collectiveness fashioned its own body in the form of Virāj. And now[1] it is intended to explain (this) creation by him.[2] [152]

[1]That is; after the creation of the gross creation.

[2]To add hereafter: In the passage *tasyām aśrāmyat...niravartatāgniḥ* (BU 1.2.2). In this is established the connection of the Sūtrātman and the world of experience.

श्रान्तस्येति तु देहस्य कर्मायोग्यत्वमुच्यते ॥
श्रमहेतुरतस्तापस्तप्तस्येत्यभिशब्द्यते ॥ १५३ ॥

But in (the adjective) *śrāntasya* is expressed the unsuitability of the body for the act (of creation), viz. the cause of fatigue (and), therefore, in the adjective *taptasya* is expressed *tāpa*, i.e. heat. [153]

This explains *tasya taptasya śrāntasya* (BU 1.2.2).

भास्वज्ज्ञानं भवेत्तेजो रसः प्राणो विवक्षितः ॥
क्रियाविज्ञानशक्तित्वात्प्रकृतस्य प्रजापतेः ॥ १५४ ॥

[Now, the significance of *tejo rasaḥ* is mentioned.]

tejo rasaḥ means brilliant knowledge—(by that) is intended Prāṇa—this is used of Prajāpati[1] (who is) the subject of this section, on account of his being possessed of the capacity for activity and knowledge. [154]

[1]Prajāpati is the Sūtrātman, the creator.

अनवच्छिन्नवपुषः पिण्डावच्छेदहेतुतः ॥
खस्य कुम्भादिनेवासोर्निरवर्तत शब्दनम् ॥ १५५ ॥

Because of the delimitation in a body of Prāṇa[1], whose body was not delimited, in the same way as (the expanse) of the sky by a pot etc.[2], there is the use of the word *niravartata* 'came forth'. [155]

[1]Sureśvara uses the word *asu* (normally used in the plural) in the sense Prāṇa, the Jīvātman.

[2]As sky is only one and yet becomes varied or divided as *ghaṭākāśa, karakākāśa, gṛhākāśa* etc.

नामरूपादिमद्देहसंबन्धात्तद्विधर्मकः ॥
अरूपोऽपि हि सूत्रात्मा लक्ष्यते रूपवानिव ॥ १५६ ॥

On account of his connection with a body that has a name, form etc.[1] the Sūtrātman, though possessed of their (entirely) opposite properties[2] and even without a form[3], is seen like one possessed of some form. [156]

[1]The word *api* implies *karman.*

[2]That is to say; it is *anāmaka, arūpaka* and *akāraka.*

[3]This indicates *anāmaka* also (SP); this justifies the reference to *nāmarūpādimattva.*

सूक्ष्मस्थूलशरीराभ्यां चिदाभाभ्यामविद्यया ॥
संवृतः परमेशोऽपि त्रैलोक्यात्माग्निरुच्यते ॥ १५७ ॥

The highest Lord, the self of the three worlds though he is, is called Agni, since he is wrapped by ignorance and by the two-fold bodies, viz. the subtle and the gross, which have the appearance of Sentience. [157]

अशरीरं शरीरेष्वनवस्थेष्ववस्थितम् ॥
महान्तं विभुमात्मानं मत्वा धीरो न शोचति ॥ १५८ ॥

"A wise man (then) pondering over (the nature of) Ātman which is without a body, which is (somehow) delimited in impermanent (i.e. perishable) bodies, the great one and the all-pervader, does not have to sorrow." [158]

This is quoted from *Kaṭhopaniṣad* 2.22.

विराड्देहावनद्धोऽसुरध्यात्माद्याधिगः खवत् ॥
व्यष्टितामेति तद्धीनः समष्टित्वेन तिष्ठति ॥ १५९ ॥

Prāṇa, (when) bound by the body of Virāj, (thus) coming under (lit. entering into) limitations[1], viz. *adhyātma* etc.[2] comes to possess individuality[3], just in the same way as a sky (becomes manifold in form)[4]. (But) (when it becomes) devoid of them (i.e. limiting adjuncts), it remains as collectivity. [159]

[1]*ādhi* is short for *upādhi* 'adjunct'.

[2]The word 'etc.' stands for *adhidaiva* and *adhibhūta*; cf. verse 127 above.

[3]Cf. note under verse 155.

[4]That is to say; comes to exist as many discrete individuals.

A man does some work, he gets exhausted, wants to rest and feels that he has done something. In the same way, Sureśvara points out, there are doings of Prāṇa, i.e. embodied Brahman.

उर्व्यामुत्पादितायां तु श्रमात्तापात्प्रजापतेः ॥
निरवर्ततेवास्यात्मा परिच्छेदाभिमानतः ॥ १६० ॥

Owing to the fatigue and heat (which he experienced) when the earth[1] was created, the self of Prajāpati became happy[2], as it were, on account of the (egoistic) feeling for the limitation, (viz. the body). [160]

[1]Sureśvara at times uses a synonym (or, synonyms) for the word in the Śruti. Thus, we come across the words *sṛṣṭi*, *pṛthivī*, *urvī* which signify the entire creation—not merely the earth.

[2]The word *niravartata* here has a sense different from that in verse 155 above. *niravarta* here is related to *nirvṛti* 'absolute joy or great joy', cf. also *nirvāṇa*, *niravartata* in that verse meant 'came forth'.

स्थूलदेहपरिच्छिन्नः स एवाद्यः प्रजापतिः ॥
अग्निरेष यतस्तस्मादुपास्योऽयं प्रयत्नतः ॥ १६१ ॥

[This verse reaffirms the thought in BUB on *teja eva rasa*. . .]

Since the very first Prajāpati, being delimited by a gross body[1], is this Agni[2], therefore, he has to be worshipped by one with (every) effort. [161]

[1]Even the minutest (i.e. the most subtle) body could be considered as gross because it has some magnitude.

[2]See verse 157.

स वै शरीरी प्रथमः स वै पुरुष उच्यते ॥
आदिकर्ता स भूतानां ब्रह्माग्रे समवर्तत ॥ १६२ ॥

"Verily he is the first embodied form (of the Brahman); verily he is called Puruṣa; he is the first creator of elements[1], (for) the god Brahmā existed in the beginning (of creation[2])." [162]

SP and NKL report this to be a verse from a *Purāṇa*. This verse is (i) identical with *Mārkaṇḍeya Purāṇa* 45.64 and *Vāyu Purāṇa* 1.4.69 and (ii) closely similar to:

Brahmāṇḍa Purāṇa 1.3.25:

sa vai śarīrī prathamaḥ purā puruṣa ucyate|
ādikartā sa bhūtānāṁ brahmā'gre samavartata||

and *Saura Purāṇa* 21.22:

sarvaiḥ śarīraiḥ prathamaḥ sa vai puruṣa ucyate|
ādikartā sa bhūtānāṁ brahmāgre samavartata||

Sureśvara mixes up Purāṇic names of the creator with the name Sūtrātman, the Prajāpati.

[1]These are thus various names/descriptions of but one creator.
[2]That is to say; before the creator attained individuality in every being.

अनुपाख्यतनुः सोऽयं व्यवहारप्रसिद्धये ॥
आत्मानं व्यभजत्स्थूलैस्त्रिधा वाय्वग्निभानुभिः ॥ १६३ ॥

[Verses 163-168 explain BU 1.2.3: The threefold division of Prajāpati and (his) worship.]

The known one, this (Ātman), who is possessed of an indescribable form (lit. body), differentiated (i.e. multiplied) himself into three forms, viz. in the three gross (form), the wind, the fire and the sun, in order that worldly dealings[1] became possible. [163]

[1]These are Upāsanā etc. SP mentions that Prajāpati's subtle body did not comprise of five gross elements, and was therefore incapable of worldly dealings.

स्वरूपानुपमर्देन स विराड्देवतात्मभिः ।।
उपासनादिसिद्ध्यर्थमात्मानं व्यभजत्स्वयम् ।। १६४ ।।

[This is the first, viz. *prima facie*, view on the preceding verse.]

That Virāj divided itself on his own, in the form of various divinities[1], without destroying its own nature in order that different (sorts of) worship etc.[2] become established. [164]

[1]Cf. *vāyvagnibhānubhiḥ* in the preceding verse.
[2]The word 'etc.' refers to various activities connected with worship.

मूलात्मैव त्रिधात्मानमभिनत्स प्रजापतिः ।।
इत्यस्य प्रतिपत्त्यर्थं स एष इति भण्यते ।। १६५ ।।

[This is the other view, viz. Siddhānta view, on verse 163.]

It is stated in the Śruti: *sa eṣa*...[1], that, in order that one understands that it is Prajāpati, the prime Ātman, who, on his own, differentiated himself. [165]

[1]This part of the Śruti together with the initial part, viz. *sa tredhātmānam vyakuruta* points but to two complementary views regarding creation.

तस्य प्रथमजस्याग्नेर्विराजोऽर्कस्य वाजिवत् ।।
दर्शनस्य विधानार्थं तस्य प्राचीति कीर्त्यते ।। १६६ ।।

(Now) it is stated (in the Śruti) *tasya prāci*...for the purpose of laying down the worship of that first born Agni, (also called) Virāj (and) Arka, as (that) of the horse[1]. [166]

[1]*vājivat* = *vājinaḥ darśanam iva* (= *upāsanam iva*); cf. Pāṇini: *tatra tasyeva-darśana* is equivalent to *upāsana* (cf. BUBV 1.1), and therefore, *vājinaḥ upāsana* means *vājimedha*, i.e. *aśvamedha*. This refers to *agnau vājidṛṣṭiḥ* (as discussed in BU 1.1).

यस्मात्कारणमुल्लङ्घ्य कार्यं नान्यत्र वर्तते ॥
अप्सु कारणभूतासु तस्मादग्निः प्रतिष्ठितः ॥ १६७ ॥

[This explains *sa eṣo 'psu pratiṣṭhitaḥ* in BU 1.2.3.]

Since an effect does not (ever) exist elsewhere, going beyond its own cause, therefore, Agni has established himself (i.e. stays) in the waters[1] which have been its cause. [167]

AnSS edition needs correction of *ulaṅghya* to *ullaṅghya*.

[1]SP points out that *apsu* stands for *bhūtāntarasahitāsu apsu*, i.e. in waters together with other elements, and *sūtrarūpāsu* 'in those having (now) the form of the Sūtrātman'.

अप्प्रतिष्ठागुणं देवमुपास्ते योऽनिशं नरः ॥
यत्र क्व चैति तत्रासौ प्रतिष्ठां लभते शुभाम् ॥ १६८ ॥

[This is the *phalaśruti* in *yatra kva ca*...in BU 1.2.3.]

Whichsoever a man ever worships the god whose characteristic is his being firmly established in waters, obtains auspicious steadiness[1] (in life) wherever he might go. [168]

[1]'which is uncensured, i.e. praise-worthy, and also unopposed (even) in the yonder world' (SP).

योऽबादिपरिपाट्यैवं विराजमसृजत्स्वयम् ॥
कीदृग्व्यापारसंयुक्तः सोऽस्त्राक्षीदिति भण्यते ॥ १६९ ॥

[Now follows the narrative of the birth of Āditya as Saṁvatsara.]

(Now) it is stated in the Śruti, 'he created...'[1] in order to explain with what kind of activities is connected he[2] who, on his own, created Virāj[3] in the succession of waters etc.[4] [169]

[1]This is reference to the connection of BU 1.2.3 and BU 1.2.4 as stated in BUB. BUBV uses *asrākṣīt* for *asṛjata* in BUB.

[2]This refers to Mṛtyu who has not differentiated himself in the five-fold elements (*apañcikṛtaprapañcātman*).

[3]Virāj is of the nature of the five-fold elements and their effects (*pañcīkṛtabhūtapañcakatatkāryasṛṣṭikramātmaka*).

[4]The word 'etc.' refers to Pṛthivī.

अत्तृसर्गोऽथवोक्तः प्रागन्नसर्गोऽधुनोच्यते ॥
अशनायावतो यस्मान्नास्त्यन्नविरहात्स्थितिः ॥ १७० ॥

[Now follows some *udbhāṣya* writing of Sureśvara regarding the connection between BU 1.2.3 and BU 1.2.4.]

Or there has been stated in (the earlier part of) the Śruti the creation of Eaters (viz. the divinities, Agni etc.) and now is stated the creation of the eatable(s) since there is no existence possible of one who has hunger in the absence of food.[1] [170]

[1]This explanation keeps in view the sentence *kanīyo 'nnaṁ kariṣye* in BU 1.2.5—this is for the Eater (*attṛ*) who was mentioned in *tejo raso niravartata* in BU 1.2.2 above.

त्रेधा व्यभजदात्मानमित्येतद्वा प्रदर्श्यते ॥
अग्निप्राणौ पुरैवोक्तावथ संवत्सरोद्भवः ॥ १७१ ॥

Or now is shown (the completion of the meaning of) the sentence 'He differentiated himself into three (forms)'[1] (thus:) Agni and Prāṇa (as being born of the Sūtrātman) have been mentioned before[2] and now (is mentioned) the birth of Saṁvatsara[3]. [171]

[1]Cf. verse 163 above.

[2]Cf. *niravartatāgniḥ* in BU 1.2.2 and *vāyaṁ tṛtīyam* in BU 1.2.3.

[3]This signifies Āditya owing to his most intimate connection with the year. This refers to BU 1.2.3: *ādityaṁ tṛtīyam.*

मनसा ज्ञाननिर्देशस्त्रयी वागिति भण्यते ॥
सर्गक्रमं स वेदोक्तं ज्ञानेनालोचयत्प्रभुः ॥ १७२ ॥

[Now (i.e. after two different explanations of the connections between BU 1.2.2-3 and BU 1.2.4), follows the meaning of *sa manasā vācaṁ mithunaṁ samabhavat* (BU 1.2.4).]

In the word *manasā* there is reference to Knowledge (and) in the word *vāk* to the three Vedas. That Lord (viz. the Sūtrātman) thought[1] with (the power of) His (excellent) knowledge of the successive order of creation that is mentioned in the Veda. [172]

[1]Cf. BU 1.2.5: *sa aikṣata...*

ज्ञानेनाप्रतिघेनासौ वेदोक्तां सृष्टिपद्धतिम् ॥
समन्वालोचयच्छंभुः सिसृक्षुर्विविधं जगत् ॥ १७३ ॥

[This is a paraphrase of Manu's verse.]

(Indeed) that origin of bliss[1] well (*sam*) thought about the successive order of creation, mentioned in the Veda, by means of his unobstructed[2] (power of) knowledge, (when he became) desirous of creating (this) manifold universe. [173]

[1]*śambhu* is said of the Lord in order to convey the idea of His compassion for the beings. He proposed to create.

[2]Cf. SP. *jñānam apratighaṁ yasya*...(quotation not traceable)

आलोच्यालोचकयोर्हि योगो मिथुनमुच्यते ॥
प्रसिद्धं मिथुनं चात्र न कथंचन युज्यते ॥ १७४ ॥

(By the use of) the word union (lit. couple)[1] is mentioned the connection of what is to be thought about and the thinker. The union (lit. couple), which is so well known in this (world) is in no way connected in this context.[2] [174]

[1]In the sentence *sa manasā vācam mithunaṁ samabhavat.*

[2]Here the context is of the embodied self (*adhyātmaprakaraṇa*); the idea of man and woman is entirely irrelavant in this context.

अनन्तराग्निसंबन्धप्रसङ्गविनिवृत्तये ॥
अशनायेति हि प्राह मूलकारणसंगतिम् ॥ १७५ ॥

[The verse explains the association of Mṛtyu and Aśanāyā.]

The Śruti has used the word *aśanāyā*[1] as going with the prime cause (of creation) for warding off the contingency of the connection with Agni[2] which is immediately (mentioned) before. [175]

[1]The word *aśanāyā* (f.) 'desire for food' is used in apposition to *mṛtyu* (m.) as its qualifier. This is in the Vedic style. Also cf. *aśanāyayā lakṣito mṛtyuḥ* (BUB p. 34).

[2]The reference to Agni is to emphasize the connection of *aśanāyā* with only the prime cause, the Sūtrātman, and not with Virāj.

जगतः प्रक्रियाबीजं यदवैषीत्पुरा गृही ॥
द्वैतैकत्वात्मकं ज्ञानं कर्म च ज्ञानसंभृतम् ॥
भावना च तयोरेतत्त्रयं रेतोऽभिधीयते ॥ १७६ ॥

[This verse explains the word *retaḥ* of the sentence BU 1.2.4: *tad yad reta āsīt.*]

The seed in the process (of creation) of the world[1] which the householder has understood formerly[2], is mentioned (in the Śruti passage, *tad yad retaḥ*) as the generative seed, viz. this triad (i) knowledge of the oneness in duality, (ii) activity performed together with (possession of) knowledge, and (iii) the impulse caused by the two. [176]

[1]This is *sṛṣṭikāraṇa* 'the cause of creation'.

[2]While he was trying to get to know the origin of creation with the help of Śāstra, that is to say; in his *sādhakāvasthā* (SP).

सृष्ट्यालोचनहेत्वेतत्सृष्टावाविरभूद्विभोः ॥
तद्भावभाव्यपः सृष्ट्वा रेतोबीजेन स प्रभुः ॥ १७७ ॥

सर्वलोकैकबीजेन गर्भ्यण्डेन बभूव ह ॥
अप एव ससर्जादौ तासु वीर्यमवासृजत् ॥ १७८ ॥

तदण्डमभवद्धैमं सहस्रांशुसमप्रभम् ॥
इत्येवं मनुनाप्युक्तः श्रौतोऽयं सर्गविस्तरः ॥ १७९ ॥

This (triad), the cause for His thinking about the creation, dawned on the All-pervader at the time of creation. Then, by means of that generative seed, that Lord, who was going to effect the creation, having (first) created waters, became possessed of a foetus within him by the unique seed of all the worlds, viz. the egg. [177]

Thus, viz. this long (narrative of) the creation mentioned in the Śruti, is stated by Manu[1] also: "Verily he first created waters and in them he released his generative seed; that golden egg became possessed of a lustre similar to that of the Sun (lit. one of thousand rays)." [178-179]

[1]Cf. *Manusmṛti* 1.8[cd] and 1.9[ab].

आपो ह वा इति तथा ह्ययमेव क्रमः श्रुतौ ॥
ज्ञानकर्मादिबीजस्य गर्भ एवं प्रजापतेः ॥ १८० ॥

So also, this very successive order of creation is (stated) in the Śruti[1] which begins with (the words) *āpo ha vā...*, and in the same way is the foetus within Prajāpati formed from the seed for knowledge, activity etc.[2] (described). [180]

[1]The verse is once again a reference to *Śatapathabrāhmaṇa*; cf. verse 151 above. Also cf. Taittirīya Br. 1.1.3.5; 1.5.2.5 and Jaiminīya Br. III. 318; Jaiminīya Upa. Br. I.56-1.

[2]The word 'etc.' stands for *bhāvanā* 'impulse' mentioned in verse 176 above.

स संवत्सरोऽभवदिति परिमाणोऽयमुच्यते ॥
अशनायादिमत्त्वात्स स्वभावबलचोदितः ॥ १८१ ॥

सृष्ट्वाद्यं घस्मरः पुत्रं तमभिव्याददात्क्षुधा ॥
भिनत्ति सर्वमर्यादां नान्वयाद्यप्यपेक्षते ॥ १८२ ॥

अस्य दग्धोदरस्यार्थे को न कुर्यादसांप्रतम् ॥ १८३ ॥

In the sentence *sa saṁvatsaro 'bhavat*, this one is stated to be the measurer (of the products). (Then), on account of having hunger etc.[1], (and) being impelled by the force of his own nature, [181]

the devourer (lit. voracious) first created his first son, (and), out of hunger, opened his mouth towards him (i.e. to devour him). (Let it not be understood that) he sets aside all bounds of morality, (for) he does not pay heed to (lit. expect) what follows etc.[2] [182]

(Indeed) what man would not do wrong for the sake of this wretched stomach[3]? [183]

[1]The word 'etc.' refers to thirst.

[2]The word 'etc.' refers to food and various enjoyments which are to follow.

[3]This is to justify the creator's voracity. SP remarks: *kṣutpipāsāpīḍitaḥ putram api bhakṣayati* and also *vivekinām api paśvādibhir aviśeṣo vyavahāradaśāyām iti bhāvaḥ.*

अन्न एव यतो वृत्तिरत्तुरन्नाद एव च ॥
अन्नस्य युक्तमेवातस्तमभिव्याददादिति ॥ १८४ ॥

Since existence of an eater (depends) on food and (the purpose of) food also (depends) on the eater[1], it is only proper, therefore, (that the Śruti) has stated 'he (the creator) opened his mouth towards him (i.e. son)'. [184]

[1]The purpose is achieved by satisfying his hunger.

जन्मान्तरसमभ्यस्तविद्याकर्मादिहेतुतः ॥
जन्यकर्मप्रयुक्तः सञ्शिशुर्भाणित्यथाकरोत् ॥ १८५ ॥

(Then[1]), on account of the lores and action etc.[2] which he has studied in his previous birth(s), the baby boy, being impelled by the activity to be performed,[3] uttered the sound *Bhāṇ*[4]. [185]

[1]Or, at that time.

[2]The word 'etc.' refers to the impressions or desires of the previous birth(s).

[3]In the explanation here the baby boy which was produced by the Sūtrātman is described as any young one of human species who is wrapped in ignorance caused by action in the past lives.

[4]Cf. SP: *asaṁskṛtaśabdakaraṇe hetvantaram āha śiśur iti.*

यथोक्तहेतुवशगः स्वभावप्रहितोऽप्यसुः ॥
कुमारोत्थरवत्रस्तः स्वभावं चिच्छिदे भयात् ॥ १८६ ॥

And Prāṇa[1], being under the sway of the already stated cause and also being urged by (his own) nature, was disturbed by the cry coming from the young boy, and turned away from[2] his own nature[3], out of apprehension. [186]

[1]Or, Mṛtyu.

[2]That is to say; gave up or lit. cut himself away from.

[3]Namely, his cruelty.

अत्यन्तमपि शूराणां स्वस्वभावैकहेतुतः ॥
तित्तिरादिसमुत्पाते वेपथुर्जायते भयात् ॥ १८७ ॥

[This states the reason for the apprehension mentioned in the preceding verse.]

Verily (do we see that) even singularly brave men go in

tremor, out of fear, only by dint of their very nature[2], when there suddenly comes a Tittira[1] or another (similar) bird. [187]

[1]This refers to the superstition that the note of a Tittira (or some such) bird portends evil.

[2]That is, by the deep-rooted fear which is so natural to human beings.

एवं स शिशुसंरावसंलब्धालोचनक्षणः ॥
ऐक्षतेह न कामार्तः कश्चिदालोचने क्षमः ॥ १८८ ॥

[Verses 188-196 explain BU 1.2.5: *sa aikṣata.*]

Thus he, who had now got (lit. obtained) a moment for thought owing to the cry of the baby boy, thought[1] (i.e. paused to think). Indeed no person who is overcome by desire (for food) is capable of (waiting for) a thought.[2] [188]

[1]Sureśvara emphasizes that the Sūtrātman paused to think even if he was hungry.

[2]Cp. the popular adage: *bubhukṣitaḥ kiṁ na karoti pāpam* 'what wrong would he not do who is hungry?' Sureśvara suggests Prajāpati's great power of thought and also the great force in the young one's cry.

मन्यतिश्चाभिपूर्वोऽयं हिंसार्थः स्यात्प्रसिद्धितः ॥
यदीममभिहिंसिष्ये कनीयोऽन्नं भवेद्ध्रुवम् ॥ १८९ ॥

[This is on the Bhāṣya: *abhipūrvo manyatiḥ.*]

This (use of) root *man* preceded by (the preposition) *abhi* is in the sense of *hiṁsā* 'destroying, violence'—for, it is (so known) from the established (usage).[1] (Therefore, the Śruti statement means:) 'If I shall kill this one, food will certainly be less.'[2] [189]

[1]NKL remarks that this meaning of the root *abhiman* is not sanctioned by (grammatical) authority. Both SP and NKL

point out (as the basis for this usage) the Śruti statements: *rudro 'sya paśūn abhimanyeta/nāsya rudraḥ paśūn abhimanyate/paśūn nābhimanyate/paśūn nābhimaṁsyate,* and *tato vai rudraḥ paśūn nābhyamanyata.*

[2]This is the meaning of *yadi vā imam abhimaṁsye kanīyo 'nnaṁ kariṣye* (BU 1.2.5).

कारणादल्पमेव स्यात्तद्व्याप्तेरदितिर्यतः ॥
अन्नमल्पं ततोऽप्यल्पात्कनीयोऽन्नं भवेदतः ॥ १९० ॥

[This supplies consideration in Prajāpati's remark in the second line of the preceding verse.]

(Again), that (food)[1] would be positively less than its cause, on account of its pervasion (by the Sūtrātman), since (the Sūtrātman) is 'Unbound'[2]. And therefore food would be less than that, (viz. the baby boy) who is already small. As such, food will indeed be less. [190]

[1]Though *tat* is translated here as food, it really refers to its cause, viz. Virāj. As such, if the Sūtrātman were to devour Virāj, then there would not follow its product, viz. food. Therefore, it is smaller than what is already small—Virāj who is, as compared to the Sūtrātman, smaller since that is an effect and therefore smaller than the cause.

[2]The Sūtrātman is called also Aditi as known from the Śruti: *adirir dyaur aditir antarikṣam...* (SP). We have 'unbound' (i.e. limitless) as the translation of the word *aditi* and we thereby refer to the Sūtrātman which amplifies itself into all products, i.e. the universe. Yet Sureśvara seems to derive the name *aditi* from root *ad* 'to eat' to signify 'eater, devourer', cf. verse 194 below. Śaṅkara says regarding the derivation of Aditi at the end of BUB 1.2.5: *mṛtyoḥ prajāpateḥ sarvasyādanād adititvaṁ veda tasyaitat phalaṁ/*

लोकेऽपीदं सुप्रसिद्धमाङ्गनाबालपण्डितम् ॥
जग्धनिःशेषबीजस्य तत्फलं नाप्यतेऽण्वपि ॥ १९१ ॥

[This is to justify the less quantity of food as stated in verse

190. That is to say: in the absence of Virāj, no food could be possible (cf. *sthūṇānikhananyāya*).]

Even in the common-place world, among all people—right from women and children upto the learned—it is well known that the product of what has its entire seed eaten up (i.e. destroyed) would not be obtained even in the least measure. [191]

कुमारवक्त्रोद्गतया वाचर्गादीन्ससर्ज सः ॥
पश्वादींश्च कुमारेण ह्यात्मनाजीजनज्जगत् ॥ १९२ ॥

[This explains *sa tayā vācā*...(BU 1.2.5.).]

He (i.e. the Sūtrātman) produced *ṛc*[1] etc. by the word uttered from the baby boy's mouth and also (produced) animals etc.[2] (and) this universe from the self, viz. the baby boy[3]. [192]

[1]This seems to indicate the origin of all expressions of speech in the baby boy's cry *Bhāṇ*.

[2]This refers to birds, crawling beings and other creatures.

[3]The identity of the cause and the effect is implied in the *sāmānādhikaraṇya* of *kumāreṇa ātmanā* 'the self, the baby boy'. This explanation is Sureśvara's variance with Śaṅkara. Read foot-note 2 on NKL (p. 50): ..*bhāṣyavyākhyānaṁ kliṣṭam iti matvā/ kleśam anudbhāvya/vārtikakāraiḥ 'vācā' ity asya prakṛtakumāramukha-nirgatavākparatvam/'ātmanā' ity asya prakṛtakumāraparatvaṁ ca varṇitam iti bodhyam.*

स्रष्टृत्त्रोः कार्यभक्ष्याभ्यामन्योन्याव्यतिरेकतः ॥
स्रष्टृत्वात्स सृजत्येव खाद्यतेऽन्नं सदाद्यतः ॥ १९३ ॥

Since the creator and the eater, as also the effects produced (by the creator) and the food to be eaten (by the eater), do not exist apart from each other, he (the Sūtrātman), because of his capacity of being the creator, does create the food and it (also) is ever eaten while the eater is eating. [193]

This brushes aside a possible doubt that the creator and the eater are different—the doubt implies that, if they were one, there would not be any increase in food. But the Upaniṣadic description does emphasize the apparent paradox.

सर्वमत्ति यतः सृष्टं तस्माददितिरुच्यते ॥
नामज्ञस्तमुपासीनः सर्वस्यात्तादितिर्भवेत् ॥ १९४ ॥

[This explains *aditer adititvam* (BU 1.2.5).]

Since he devours all that is created, he is called Aditi. One who knows the (significance of this) name, worshipping him (lit. seated nearmost unto him) would himself become Aditi, the eater of all.[1] [194]

[1]This points to the significance of Upāsanā, as SP points out in *yathopāsanaṁ hi phalam*. Also read NKL (last note on p. 50): *sarvasyaitasya jagato 'nnabhūtasya attā sarvātmanaiva bhavati/ anyathā virodhāt/na hi sarvasya kaścid eko 'ttā dṛśyate/tasmāt sarvātmā bhavatīty arthaḥ/*

सर्वात्तृत्वेन सिद्धेऽर्थे सर्वान्नोक्तिः किमीर्यते ॥
अन्नमेव भवेदन्नं नान्नमत्तस्य कुत्रचित् ॥ १९५ ॥

[This explanation averts the notion of repetition in respect of *sarvasyaitasyāttā bhavati/sarvam asyānnam bhavati* (BU 1.2.5).]

Why is there the statement: 'all (becomes His) food,' when (that) fact is (already) established by (the mention of Him as) capable of being the eater of all? (The purpose of so saying is to affirm:) Food alone becomes the food for the eater and nowhere does the food become the eater of this one (viz. the eater). [195]

प्राणात्मात्तैव सोऽवश्यमुपासनबलाद्भवेत् ॥
य एवमभिधानज्ञ उपासीतादितिं सदा ॥ १९६ ॥

[This is reaffirmation of the *phalaśruti* (cf. verse 194 above) as in *ya evam*...(BU 1.2.5).]

He, who is thus the knower (of the meaning) of the name Aditi, should ever worship Aditi; (for) certainly he will be (i.e. become possessed) of the nature of Prāṇa, the very eater (of every eatable), owing to the excellence of the worship. [196]

अश्वाश्वमेधनाम्नोऽथ कारणप्रतिपत्तये ॥
सोऽकामयत इत्यादिः परो ग्रन्थोऽवतार्यते ॥ १९७ ॥

[Verses 197-205 explain the meaning of the word *aśva* (BU 1.2.6).]

Now is introduced the later section (of the Upaniṣad), beginning with (the words) 'he desired...'[1] in order that one comes to know the reason (why Prajāpati has) the name Aśva and Aśvamedha[2] (for Prajāpati). [197]

[1]Sureśvara does not intend the Saṁdhi of *so 'kāmayata* and *iti* (as *°yateti*).

[2]These names are explained etymologically in verses 208 and 209 below. The use of the singular form *aśvāśvamedhanāmnaḥ* indicates the oneness of *aśva* and *aśvamedha* which is implied and emphasized.

यज्ञेन भूयसा यक्ष्य इत्येवं स प्रजापतिः ॥
अश्वमेधो भवेद्भूयान्भूयोदक्षिणको हि सः ॥ १९८ ॥

'Let me perform the great[1] sacrifice,' thus (thought) that Prajāpati; that great (sacrifice) could be (only) the Aśvamedha since (it) involves great (i.e. amount of) Dakṣiṇā 'fees to be given to the priest'.[2] [198]

[1]'great', because it is *bhūyodakṣiṇāka* as BUB explains and the next line points out. This is use of *significant* adjective (constituting the figure of speech Kāvyaliṅga).

[2]SP refers to the prescription of *Āpastamba Śrauta Sūtra*: (where?) *prācyādidikcatuṣṭayasyādhvaryuprabhṛtibhyaś caturbhyo bhūmya vacchinnasya cāvaśiṣṭasya dhanasya sadasyebhyo dakṣiṇātvena deyatā.*

यजेय भूयोऽपीत्येवमकामयत भावितः ॥
ऋत्वात्मेत्यभिमानेद्धः पूर्वजन्मन्यभूत्प्रभुः ॥ १९९ ॥

Prajāpati, inspired (by the performance) desired, 'Let me perform (that sacrifice) once again', since in his previous life the Lord was kindled with the pride: 'I am the soul of the sacrifice.' [199]

This presupposes the continued cycle of births for Prajāpati; since he had an Ego that he was the performer or maker of the sacrifice. This naturally leads to the Upaniṣadic idea of the working of *mayā* in the form of one's entertaining the notion that one is the agent of so many ritualistic activities. Also it entails the notion of the Liṅgātman for every human being, just as Hiraṇyagarbha, the sacrificer, continued to have the Liṅgātman.

पूर्वजन्माभिनिर्वृत्तप्रयोगापेक्षयोच्यते ॥
भूयो यजेयेति वचः सदा तद्भावभावनात् ॥ २०० ॥

ऋत्वात्मैवाभिसंपन्नो द्वैतैकत्वात्मकः प्रभुः ॥
इह तत्फलतां यातो भूयोवाग्युग्यते ततः ॥ २०१ ॥

The statement (in the Śruti) *bhūyo yajeta* 'let me again sacrifice' is made with reference to the performance of a sacrifice accomplished in a previous life, for there would ever be its inspiration by the thought (i.e. the pride) of (having performed) it. [200]

The Lord, having only the nature of oneness in duality, became (possessed of the thought that he was) 'the soul of the sacrifice'. Thus he has here become the result of that (sacrifice) and, therefore, the word *bhūyaḥ* 'again' is used (in the Śruti)[1]. [201]

[1]SP well brings out the purport of these two verses thus: *sādhakāvasthāyāṁ dīrghakālam ādareṇa nirantaratayā hiraṇyagarbho 'smīti bhāvanāvaśād ubhayavidhakratvātmā prajāpatir eva samaṣṭivyaṣṭy-*

ātmā sampannaḥ sann etatkalpādau kratuphalatām yato yātas tato bhūyaḥśabdo yuktimān ity arthaḥ.

कारणप्रवणं सर्वं कार्यं दृष्टं जगत्यपि ॥
प्रकृतिं यान्ति भूतानि निग्रहः किं करिष्यति ॥ २०२ ॥

In the universe[1] also it is seen that all effect is dependent on the cause[2]; (so it is said in *Gītā* 3.33[3]:) 'all beings act under the influence of nature, what (then) can restraint do?' [202]

[1]This refers to *vyavahārāvasthā.*

[2]That is; Prakṛti is responsible for every performance of a human being. So then, it impels even Prajāpati to perform a sacrifice.

[3]This is the Smṛti support for the philosophical thought.

यशोवीर्यैकहेतुत्वात्प्राणा यश इहेष्यताम् ॥
यशः प्रकाशरूपेण वीर्यं तद्बलहेतुतः ॥ २०३ ॥

[This explains *prāṇā vai yaśo vīryam* (BU 1.2.6).]

Let it be understood here that *prāṇas*[1] are fame, since they are the only cause of fame and potency; fame they are, because of their being in the form of lustre or glory (i.e. known everywhere) and potency, thanks to being the cause of their strength.[2] [203]

[1]Prāṇas are organs of sense, viz. eye etc.; cf. *prāṇaś cakṣurādayaḥ* (BUB p. 39).

[2]*tadbalahetutaḥ* is *tadbalahetutvataḥ*, cf. SP *asti ca dehe teṣām balahetutvam...*

उदक्रामद्यशो वीर्यं विराजः श्रमकर्शितात् ॥
लिङ्गात्मेह यशो वीर्यमुभयं हि तदुद्भवम् ॥ २०४ ॥

[This explains *tad evaṁ yaśovīryabhūteṣu*... (BUB p. 39).]

Fame (and) potency (as well) departed from Virāj who was weakened by fatigue; for both fame and potency, originating from it, are here[1] the Liṅgātman 'the subtle self'.[2] [204]

[1]The word *iha* refers to the gross body.

[2]Read NKL: *sthūladehe prāṇasambandhe saty evea yaśo vīryaṁ nāsati ityanvayavyatirekasiddham ity arthaḥ.*

पूर्वदेहेऽभिषङ्गोऽभूदपविद्धतनोरपि ॥
सङ्गत्यागो ह्यसंभाव्यो विनैकात्म्यावबोधनात् ॥ २०५ ॥

[This explains *tasya prajāpateḥ...śarīre mana āsīt* (BUB p. 39).]

(Even at this time[1]) Prajāpati had an attachment to the body of the previous life even though he was devoid of (i.e. removed from that former) body. Indeed giving up an attachment cannot be possible (for one) without becoming aware of the oneness (of the two bodies[2]). [205]

[1]This is to be added in view of verses 199-200 above.

[2]These are: The body of the previous and the present birth. This really means the continuation of the same life in different bodies. But, even though the objects enjoyed in the earlier life do not any more exist, the longing for them persists (even in the subtle body). This is supported by SP which refers to *Gītā* 2.59: *viṣayā vinivartate nirāhārasya dehinaḥ/rasavarjaṁ...*

जातदेहाभिषङ्गः संस्तादात्म्यप्रतिपित्सया ॥
मेध्यमित्यादिकं कामं सोऽकामयत कामुकः ॥ २०६ ॥

[Verses 206-227 explain BU 1.2.7. And this verse clarifies *sa tasminn eva śarīre...* (BUB p. 39).]

Having an attachment to the body that arose (in him), he, full of longing entertained a desire for what is fit for a sacrifice etc.[1], owing to his wish to obtain oneness in nature with it. [206]

This verse stresses further the notion of *saṅga* mentioned in the preceding verse.

[1]The word *medhya* has here a reference to the body and not to offerings of sacrifice, because already a reference is made to Prajāpati's wish for becoming *ātmanvī*—it is repeated here in BU 1.2.7 also.

अपविद्धयशोवीर्यं शरीरं कवियोगतः ॥
यतोऽश्वयदतोऽश्वोऽसुः संवृत्तः स प्रजापति : ॥ २०७ ॥

(And) since the Prāṇa then swelled[1] (his) body, which was devoid of fame and potency on account of His separation from Prajāpati[2], he became a horse; (he became) Prajāpati.[3] [207]

[1]The word *aśvayat* is for a Vedic form *aśvat* from root *śvī* 'to swell, grow, increase'. Or, is it, by any chance, an archaic form of *aśvayat* from the denominative root *aśvaya* 'to act like a horse' (i.e. 'to enter like a horse')?

[2]The words '(his) body' refer to the gross manifest form of an individual sacrificer who is far removed from the status of Prajāpati, the Hiraṇyagarbha—this has reference to the disappearance of Prāṇas mentioned in verse 203 above. The verse uses the word *ka* in *kaviyogataḥ* for conveying the sense of Prajāpati in keeping with later (Upaniṣadic, or perhaps post-Upaniṣadic) tendency to do so. *kaviyoga* is understood from verse 204 above.

[3]This is said with a view to averting the idea of the non-identity of the horse in the form of the body and Prajāpati. This suggests that the horse, being Prajāpati, is worship-deserving.

व्यपेतसद्यशोवीर्यममेध्यं मेध्यतामगात् ॥
तत्प्रवेशाद्यतोऽस्तोऽयमश्वमेधोऽभवत्प्रभुः ॥ २०८ ॥

[This explains the reason for Aśvamedha to be Prajāpati's name.]

Since the body, from which (the earlier) extant fame and potency had disappeared and which had thus become unfit for sacrifice[1], (now) became fit for sacrifice owing to the entry of that (i.e. Prajāpati) (into it); for this reason, the Lord has become this[2] Aśvamedha[3]. [208]

[1]Cf. *medhya* in verse 206 above.
[2]That means 'well-known'.
[3]Cf. SP: *śarīraṁ hi prāṇaviyogāt.*

अश्वाश्वमेधावेवं च प्राजापत्यात्मनाञ्जसा ॥
अभिष्टुतौ कथं नाम भवेतामिति भण्यते ॥ २०९ ॥

(The above) is stated with a view to (explaining) how the Aśva 'horse' and Aśvamedha 'the horse-sacrifice' would become praised in a proper manner, on account of their being of the nature of Prajāpati. [209]

काललोकादिवपुषस्त्वश्वस्याग्नेश्च सांप्रतम् ॥
समस्योपासनं वाच्यमित्यर्थो ग्रन्थ उत्तरः ॥ २१० ॥

[This explains the purpose of *eṣa ha vā aśvamedham* (BU 1.2.7).]

(Now) it is proper to prescribe (lit. state) the worship together of the horse, which has a body comprising of time, region etc.[1], and Fire together—therefore, for this purpose, follows the subsequent (part of the) work.[2] [210]

[1]This refers to the contents of BU 1.1.1. The word 'etc.' refers to the deity (of the sacrifice).

[2]In BU 1.1.1 there was discussion of the worship of the horse; there was no mention of the worship of fire. Therefore, the section in BU which begins with *na ha vā aśvamedham* has the purpose of showing that the two so-called worships are not different and that they together form but one worship.

विधायकपदाभावादसंगानं परस्परम् ॥
पदानामिति मा प्रापदित्यर्थेयं परा श्रुतिः ॥ २११ ॥

[This verse explains the purpose of the injunction *aśvamedhaṁ veda* (BU 1.2.7).]

This later Śruti[1] proceeds indeed for the purpose of averting the undesirable contingent situation that the words (Aśva and Agni), which might not go together with each other owing to the absence of such words as prescribe (the worship of) Aśva.[2] [211]

Hereby is bridged over the apparent distance between ritual and philosophy. The purpose of the following passages is to assert that the worship of Aśva and the worship of Fire are not two different worships.

[1]The injunction: *aśvamedhaṁ veda.*

[2]SP and NKL point out that, though the words *adititvaṁ veda* are noticed in respect of the worship of Aśva (BU 1.2.5), they are not *pradhānavidhi* which is desired to be stated. Cf. also Ānandagiri on BUB: *pūrvatra kriyāpadasya...iti bhāvaḥ* (p. 39).

एष एवं यथातत्त्वमश्वमेधं विवेद यः ॥
वक्ष्यमाणेन रूपेण वेद विद्यादतस्तथा ॥ २१२ ॥

[This verse connects *ya enam evaṁ veda* with the injunction kept in view by the preceding verse and gives the full meaning intended, viz. 'he should know the Aśvamedha according to the description which follows.']

He, who has thus known the Aśvamedha in its true nature and also as having that nature which will be described (hereafter), should therefore know (the same) accordingly[1]. [212]

[1]According to the description which follows.

आत्मानमश्वं संकल्प्य काललोकादिधर्मिणम् ॥
तथाविधशरीरः सन्सर्वलोकपितामहः ॥ २१३ ॥

यजेयमश्वमेधेन भूयोऽपीत्यभ्यमन्यत ॥
भूर्लोकाद्यात्मकं सोऽश्वमात्मानं निरवग्रहम् ॥ २१४ ॥

यावदब्दं मुमोचाश्वं स्वच्छन्दं मुक्तबन्धनम् ॥
ततः संवत्सरादूर्ध्वं तं चाप्यालभतात्मने ॥ २१५ ॥

[The following well compares with *aśvadṛṣṭi* etc. in BUBV 1.1—this is *aśvamedhadṛṣṭi* on the same pattern.]

Having formed a notion about his own body[1] as the horse, possessed of the properties of *kāla*, *loka* etc.[2] and being possessed of that kind of body[3], the grandfather of all the world thought to himself, [213]

'Let me perform the Aśvamedha once again.' Then he let loose himself, a horse, who is possessed of the nature of earth, *lokas* etc. (and) who has no restraint whatever, [214]

till the end of the year, (to move about) according to its sweet will and without any check. Then, after a year was over, he killed that (horse) also for his own sake. [215]

[1]The word *ātman* here means 'body'.
[2]The word 'etc.' refers to the deity as in verse 210 above.
[3]A body on which are imposed the characteristics of *kāla*, *loka* etc.

स्वात्मावयवभूताभ्यो देवताभ्यो यथायथम् ॥
ग्राम्यारण्यान्पशून्प्रादादन्याभ्यः स प्रजापतिः ॥ २१६ ॥

[This is a comment on *paśūn devatābhyaḥ*... (BU 1.2.7).]

That Prajāpati (then) offered domestic and wild animals to the other deities as had become the limbs of his own body in one way or the other as is laid down (in the scriptures). [216]

[There follows a comment on *tasmāt sarvadevatya*... (BU 1.2.7).]

यतोऽकरोद्विराडेवं तस्मादेवेह याज्ञिकाः ॥
प्रोक्षितं सर्वदेवत्यं प्राजापत्यं तुरंगमम् ॥ २१७ ॥

आलभन्ते यतस्तस्माद्यथाव्याख्याततत्त्ववित् ॥
कुर्यादेवं यथोक्तार्थं मृत्युत्वप्रतिपित्सया ॥ २१८ ॥

[There follows a comment on *tasmāt...sarvadevatya...* (BU 1.2.7).]

Since Virāj did thus, therefore, only do the ritualists in this world kill a horse dedicated to Prajāpati (and understand as one) made up of all deities, when it is sprinkled over with water. [217]

Since (this is so,) therefore one, who knows the truth that is thus explained (in the Upaniṣad) should, with a wish (to obtain the nature of) Mṛtyu, perform the said (ritual) accoringly. [218]

कर्मोपासनमुक्त्वाऽथ तत्फलोपदिदिक्षया ॥
एष वा इति यत्नेन ह्याजगामोत्तरा श्रुतिः ॥ २१९ ॥

[Verses 219-227 are the explanation of the result of the worship of Aśvamedha.]

Having enjoined (lit. described) the nature of the activity of worship (i.e. performance of the ritual), now proceeds the later (portion of the) Śruti, with the specification: *eṣa vā...*,[1] indeed with a desire to state its result (lit. fruit). [219]

[1]That is, *eṣa ha vā...*; the word *ha* is dropped in the verse for the sake of metre.

दर्शनाद्यभिनिर्वृत्तो यस्त्वेवं हयसाधनः ॥
प्रत्यक्षं फलरूपेण स एष इति दर्श्यते ॥ २२० ॥

And (in the Śruti beginning with) *sa eṣa*...is directly pointed out as the result the one[1] that is secured by *darśana*[2] etc. and has the horse as its means (for accomplishing the desired result[3]). [220]

[1]This refers to the Sun in the sky. That is to say, the performance of Aśvamedha results into the actual worship of Āditya.

[2]The word *darśana* is nothing but *upāsanā* as seen in the be-

ginning of this Brāhmaṇa, viz. in 1.2.1 and also in 1.1.1, and the word 'etc.' means *manana*. This refers to the identification of the different parts of the ritual as the objects in the worship of fire.

[3]This refers to the actual performance of Aśvamedha.

अश्वमेधक्रियापूर्वपरिणामैकवर्त्मना ॥
अश्वमेधो रविः साक्षादुषा इत्यादिनोदितः ॥ २२१ ॥

In the Śruti beginning with *uṣā* is stated that the Sun itself is the Aśvamedha (which is accomplished[1]) by the only way of (viz. creating) *apūrva* through the performance of the Aśvamedha. [221]

SP supports the meaning of the verse by a line from *Manusmṛti*, viz. 3.76: *agnau prāstāhutiḥ samyag ādityam upatiṣṭhataḥ*...

[1]Accomplishing the performance of the Aśvamedha is performing the worship of the Sun and thereby becoming one with Him. This signifies the oneness of the *darśana* and *karman* (as in the preceding verse). Cf. NKL: (on that verse) *aśvamedhopāsanam aśvamedhaś cāditya evety arthaḥ.*

तस्य संवत्सर आत्मा तस्याऽऽदित्यैकहेतुतः ॥
तस्य क्रत्वात्मनश्चित्यो योऽङ्गभूतः पुरोदितः ॥ २२२ ॥

फलात्मकः स एवैष पार्थिवोऽग्निः प्रदर्श्यते ॥
आत्मान एते तस्यापि त्रयो लोका यथोदिताः ॥ २२३ ॥

Year is the nature of that (Sun) because it has only Āditya as its cause and that fire, which was to be collected and which has been described before as an aspect of that (Āditya) who is the form of the sacrifice, as said before, [222]

is of the nature of the result, i.e. this very terrestrial fire. So are these three worlds the forms[1] of that (Āditya) as said before. [223]

[1]*ātmanaḥ* = *śarirāvayvāḥ*; the very body which has the worlds as its limbs.

क्रतुतत्साधनात्मानावादित्याग्नी यथोदितौ ।।
निर्वृत्तात्माधिकारौ तावेकैवासौ भवेदसुः ।। २२४ ।।

As said before, Āditya and Agni, who are two forms (of the Aśvamedha), (of the sacrifice) being its means[1] and also the sacrifice, have, on performing their own duties[2], become but one, viz. the Prāṇa[3]. [224]

[1]It signifies 'by porducing the result of the performance'.

[2]Even these two deities have to perform their role in the Aśvamedha and then they attain the higher status of Prāṇa etc.

[3]The word *asu* is used here in feminine to indicate *prāṇadevatā* (f.) 'the deity of the name Prāṇa'. Or, is this a case of double saṁdhi?

अशनायावती योक्ता मृत्युः सर्वान्नघस्मरा ।।
सैवात्मा विदुषः साक्षादात्मा स्यादजरोऽमरः ।। २२५ ।।

[This explains *apa punar mṛtyuṁ jayate* (BU 1.2.7).]

(And) Mṛtyu[1], who is described as possessed of hunger and devourer of all foods, is himself the self of one who has known (the Brahman) and (also) the Ātman that would be without old age and without death. [225]

[1]Like the word *asu* in the previous verse, the word *mṛtyu* here is used in the feminine thereby to indicate *mṛtyudevatā* that is identical with the Ātman.

नैनमाध्यात्मिको मृत्युस्तन्मृत्युत्वादवाप्नुयात् ।।
सकृन्मृत्वासुदेहेन मुच्यते सर्वबन्धनात् ।। २२६ ।।

[This explains *mṛtyur asya* (BU 1.2.7).]

And since he (the learned man) is (that) Mṛtyu (himself), bodily death would not affect him[1]. Once he dies (in the usual sense), he is liberated from all bonds by his form of Prāṇa. [226]

[1]This is further described in the style of the *Brāhmaṇas* as *etāsāṁ devatānām eko bhavati* at the end of BU 1.2.7.

अग्न्यादिभेदभिन्नानां देवतानामशेषतः ॥
आत्माभिन्नो भवत्येष यथोक्तोपासनाद्बुधः ॥ २२७ ॥

[This explains *etāsāṁ devatānām...*]

By the performance of the worship as described (herein), a wise man becomes this Ātman which is non-distinct from all the deities which are differentiated by the variety (of names) Agni etc. [227]

// iti prathamādhyāyasya dvitiyam aśvamedhabrāhmaṇaṁ samāptam//

SELECT GLOSSARY

[Figure(s) in the parentheses indicate the number(s) of verses under translation. Verses of BUBV 1.2 are indicated only by the verse number, and verses of BUBV 1.1 are indicated by prefixing **1.1 to** the verse number. E.g. (100) for BUBV 1.2.100 and (1.1.3) for BUBV 1.1.3.]

akārakatva	not having the character of agent (116)
akṣavat	like direct perception (56)
agni	fire (1.1.5; 1), Agni (=Ātman, Prajāpati, Mṛtyu) (148; 149; 157; 161; 166; 167; 171; 195; 224; 227)
aṅkura	a sprout (38; 43)
aṅkurakumbhavat	like a sprout and/or a pitcher (34)
aṅga	limb (1.1.3; 1.1.4), part (1.1.3)
aja	unborn (26; 126)
ajara	without old age (225)
ajāta	not born (64)
ajñāta	not known (64)
ajñātasatattvaka	whose nature is not known (9)
ajñānādhigama	knowledge of (some earlier) unknown (object) (24)
ajñātārtha	(earlier) unknown object (23)
ajñātatvāpamārṣṭyartham	for wiping away (i.e. removal of) the unknownness (of objects)
ajñānānupamarda	non-removal (i.e. non-destruction) of Ignorance (132)
ajñānaikavyapāśraya	(that) which rests purely (i.e. solely) on Ignorance (about the Ātman) (129)
atiśaya	excellence (16; 23; 46)
atīta	past (108; 109)
atītaiṣyat	(that) which existed in the past and (that) which will exist in the future (108; 113)
attṛ	eater (195)
attṛsarga	creation of eaters (170)
aditi	Aditi 'unbound' (190; 194)
adhyātmādhidaiva	different parts of the body and (deities) superintending over them (141)

adhyātmādyādhi — limiting adjunct beginning with that which belongs to a body (159)
ananyadṛk — one unlike any other (thing) (26)
anavasthā — infinite regress (65; 86)
anaṣṭa — not destroyed, existent (69)
anāgata — future (109)
anāvaraṇatā — state of not being a cover (of another) (95)
anupalabdhi — non-perception (4; 5; 53)
anumā — reasoning (111)
anumeya — something to be inferred (31)
anutpanna — unproduced (69)
anumāna — inference (30)
antarbhāva — being included, inclusion (95)
anytaryāmin — the entrant (i.e. existent) within (131)
anonyavyatirekitva — state of having existence distinct from each other (14)
anyonyātmakatā — being of the nature of each other (14)
anyvonyāviṣayatva — not being the objects of each other (70)
anaya — continuation (51)
apaviddhātiśiti — (knowledge) which has set aside (the possibility of) any (other) excelling (knowledge) (110)
apahnuti — concealment (16)
aśitāśeṣasaṁsāra — that which has withdrawn (lit. swallowed) the entire existence (universe) (131)
apratigha — unobstructed (173)
abhāva — non-existence (17; 19; 114; 115)
abhāvatva — character of non-existence (20)
abhāvavacas — the statement of non-existence (of some defects etc.) (16)
abhidhāna — name (15)
abhivyakti — manifestation (77; 92; 97; 98)
revealing (87)
abhivyakta — manifest (77)
abhivyaktidharmatva — having the characteristic of being revealed (74)
abhisaṁvyāpti — pervasion (16)
abhīṣṭa — accepted (lit. desired) (26)
amara — without death (225)
ayutasiddhatā — character of having inseparable existence (121)
arka — Agni known as Arka (1.1.5; 147; 148; 149; 166)
arcana — Arcana, i.e. offering worship (145)
avadhṛti — (emphatic) assertion (84)
avadhyavadhimadbheda — distinction, between limitation and what is limited (in existence) (118)

avayava	limb (1.1.2)
avijñātātmayāthātmya	whose true nature has not been known (125)
avidyā	Ignorance (135; 136; 137)
aviśvāsa	want of faith (65)
avyakta	unmanifest (77)
avyaya	imperishable (126)
avyākṛta	not differentiated (131), unmanifest (143)
aśanāyādimattva	state of having hunger etc. (181)
aśanāyāvat	who is oppressed by hunger (225)
aṣṭakṣaṇāvastha	having eight states (i.e. forms) (69)
asadvastu	non-existent thing (15)
asādhāraṇarūpa	(things) having different shapes or of different forms (56)
asura	demon (159)
āgama	Āgama (i.e. Śruti), traditionally accepted scripture (30)
ātman	body (1.1.4; 144; 213; 223)
ātmanvī	being who possesses a body (144)
ātmahetuhā	destroyer of one's own cause (17)
ādikartṛ	first creator (162)
āditya	Āditya, the Sun (222; 224)
āyatana	abode (10)
āvaraṇa	covering (93)
āvaraṇabhaṅga	destroying, i.e. removal of the covering (106)
āvṛtatā	state of being covered (106)
āvṛta	covered (93)
āvṛtatva	state of being covered (96)
āvṛti	cover (88)
īśa	the Lord (1.1.9; 109; 110; 137)
īśvara	the Lord (1.1.9)
utpanna	produced (69; 92)
utpatti	origination (2; 3)
utpatsu	wanting to (i.e. about to) be produced (69)
udbhūti	rise (43)
upamarda	act of destroying (39), destruction (41)
upādāna	material (cause) (126)
upāya	means (27)
uṣas	dawn (1.1.2)
aikātmya	being of one nature (49)
aikātmyāvabodhana	becoming aware of oneness (with the Brahman) (205)
aikātmyabodhamātra	only the knowledge of uniqueness (28)
aiśvarya	capacity for effecting something (87)
kāraka	agent (116)
kāraṇa	the source or cause (1.1.9)
kāraṇatritaya	three causes (82; 85; 86)

trīṇi kāraṇāni	three causes (84)
trayaṁ kāraṇam	three causes (84)
kāryāpyayatva	state of being merged into the effect (9)
kāryotpattisthitilaya	production, existence and merger of an effect (82)
kālādi	*kāla* (its division) and other aspects (viz. *loka* 'region', *devatā*) connected with Aśvamedha sacrifice (1.1.2; 1.1.3; 1.1.4)
kālalokādivapuṣ	having forms of *kāla* and *loka* etc. (210)
kālalokādidharmin	having properties like *kāla* and *loka* etc. (213)
kūṭastha	immutable (137)
kratvātman	(being) the soul of sacrifice (1.1.6; 199; 201; 222)
krama	sequence or successive order (of creation) (180)
kriyātmatva	being of the nature of an action (116)
kriyābheda	difference between two actions (102)
kriyāvijñānaśaktitva	being the capacity for action and knowledge (154)
kriyāvijñānaśaktyātman	having of the capacity for knowledge for activity (138)
klṛpta	imagined (119)
kṣaṇika	momentary (62; 63)
kṣaṇikatva	momentariness (61; 62; 63)
kṣetrajñātṛ	knower of a field (which becomes possessed of body (*kṣetra*). (137)
gati	going (18; 42)
garbhāṇḍa	(golden) egg (178)
grasiṣṇu	devourer (126)
ghasmara	devourer (voracious) (182; 225)
cit	Sentience (157)
cityanāmārtham	for indicating the name of (fire) which is to be collected (from a suitable source) (149)
jagat	universe (1.1.9; 22; 31; 80; 126; 174; 176; 192; 202)
jagdhaṇiḥśeṣabīja	the entire seed (of which) is eaten up (191)
janimat	having a birth (39)
janma	production (lit. birth) (52)
jñāna	Knowledge (172)
jñānamātrasatattva	which is of the nature of mere knowledge (9)
jyotiḥ	fire (142)
tamas	darkness (99; 100; 104; 136)
tādātmya	oneness of something with another (1.1.6; 23)
tirobhūti	concealment (92)
tittirādi	Tittira and other birds (187)

darśana	Upāsanā (worship, lit. seeing) (1.1.1; 1; 220)
devatātman	forms of various divinities (164)
dvaitaikatvātmaka	having the nature of oneness in duality (123; 176; 201)
dvaividhya	being of two types (88; 92)
naṁṣṭṛ	destroyer (18; 42)
naṣṭa	destroyed (92)
nāśādikṛt	cause of (eight states of a thing) beginning with destruction (69)
nāśabhedaviruddhārthaprameya	object of knowledge which is opposed (in nature) to destruction or discreteness (68)
nidrā	sleep (133)
niḥ $\sqrt{}$*vṛt*	to be happy (160)
nihnuti	concealment (5)
nṛśṛṅgavat	like the horns of a human being (74)
parimāṇa	pervader (lit. measurer) (of products) (181)
piṇḍa	body (8; 155)
	a lump (44; 46; 50; 51; 52; 53; 54; 55; 57; 93)
pratijñā	enunciation (21; 22)
pratijñārtha	the thing enunciated (64)
pratiṣedha	denial (113)
pratyakṣa	direct perception (30; 58; 59; 68; 110)
	directly perceptible (46; 220)
pratykṣam	directly manifest (56)
pratyagrūpa	one having the form of inner self (of an individual) (26)
pratyabhijñā	recognition (of a thing) (61; 62; 64)
pratyarthin	opponent (68)
prabhaviṣṇu	ruler (126)
prabhu	Lord (199; 201)
pramāṇa	means of knowing (79)
pramāṇatā	status of a means of knowing (24)
pramāṇavyāpṛti	operation of a means of knowing (105)
prameya	object of knowledge (19)
prayatnataḥ	with (every) effort (161), cf. *yatna* below
prayoga	application (31)
prājāpatya	nature of Prajāpati (209; 217)
prājāpatyatva	status of being Prajāpati (1.1.1)
prāgabhāva	prior non-existence (114; 117; 1187)
prāmāṇyavat	authoritativeness (25)
prāṇādi	subtle Prāṇa and gross things of the world (2)
prāṇātman	of the nature of Prāṇa, i.e. Ātman (196)
buddhi	knowledge (62; 63; 65; 67)

brahman	God Brahmā (162)
bhāṇ	the sound Bhāṇ (185)
bhāvanā	impulse (176)
bhāvyartha	forthcoming object (112)
bhūyodakṣiṇaka	requiring large amount of fees to be given to a priest (198)
māna	means of knowing (45; 53; 54; 79; 101)
mānābheda	non-distinction from the means of knowing (23)
mānameya	means of knowledge and the object of knowing (79)
māyā	Māyā (=*avidyā*) (135)
miti	inference (45)
mithuna	union (lit. couple) (174)
mithyā	false (109)
mūlakāraṇa	prime cause (175)
mūlātman	first Ātman (165)
mṛgāmbudhi	mirage, lit. ocean perceived by a deer (in some desert) (71)
mṛṣātva	falsity (72; 73)
medhya	fit to be sacrificed (206; 208)
meyābhatva	look of an object of knowing (103)
meyābhisaṁgata	united (i.e. become one) with the object of knowledge (103)
melana	coming together or collection (85)
moha	Ignorance (lit. infatuation) (130)
yatna	effort (29; 96; 106)
	specification (140; 219)
yoga	connection (122)
labdhātmaka	that which has come into existence (88)
liṅga	cause (58)
	Inference (59)
liṅgātman	subtle Ātman (204)
vartamānaniṣedha	denying the existence of an existent (112)
vājivat	horse sacrifice (=Aśvamedha) (166)
vijñāna	idea (19)
vijñānālambanatva	being the basis of some idea (75)
vijñānamātra	mere idea (22)
vijñānāvyatirekitva	not being apart from an idea (25)
vidyā	Knowledge (146; 157)
vibhakta	discrete (objects) (95)
vibhu	(all-)pervader (145)
viruddhāvyabhicāritva	invariable opposition (59; 60)
virodhitva	being opposed (to each other) (14)
vivāda	dispute (32)
viśvakṛt	maker of all (124)

vīrya	potency (203; 204; 207; 208)
vairāja	belonging to Virāj (152)
vyaktāvyaktātman	nature or form of the manifest and the unmanifest (136)
vyapadeśa	assertion (114; 117) name (119)
vyavadhāna	obstacle to, or what covers the view (90; 104; 107)
vyavahāra	worldly dealings (89; 163)
vyaṣṭisamṣṭyātman	Brahman which assumes individual forms and a unified form (152)
vyākṛti	modification (132)
vyāpāra	activity (107)
śaktyavasthā	the state of (the Brahman, the Sūtrātman) having the capacity for creation (150)
śiśu	young one (185; 1878)
śiśuvaktṛkā	(something) spoken by a child (i.e. an ignorant person) (41)
śuddhasaṁskārāśraya	purely the abode (i.e. support) for (various) modifications (131)
samyagjñāna	true Knowledge (133)
saṁvatsara	Āditya (171; 181; 222) a year (215)
saṁvyāpti	pervasion (43)
satattva	true nature (9)
sattattvaka	having the true nature of the existent (29)
satpratiṣṭha	having the existent as support (10)
sadātman	having the nature of an existent (91)
samaṣṭitva	one unified form (159)
samudra	Samudra (1.1.9); Virāj (8; 123; 124; 125)
sambandha	relation (66; 115; 116; 119; 121) mutual relationship (14)
sarvamaryādā	all bounds (of morality) (182)
sarvavādin	Sarvāstivādin (24)
sarvaśakti	omnipotent (126)
sarvaśūnyatvavādin	Śūnyavādin, nihilist (21)
sahetuka	having a cause (19)
sthāyin	object that continues to exist (67)
svavibhūti	expansion of oneness (145)
svātmājñānaja	produced from ignorance of one's self (?)
svātmaikājñānavṛtta	effect of its own ignorance (126)
svābhāsavartman	channel of one's own appearances (127)
svābhāsānātmajanma	(Ignorance) which arises from non-self resembling itself (137)

hetu	reason (21; 22)
hetumat	having a cause (33)
hnuti	removal (lit. concealment) (100; 104)

BIBLIOGRAPHY

TEXTS

Brahmasūtraśāṅkarabhāṣya with the Commentaries Bhāmatī, Kalpataru and Parimala, Bombay : Nirnaya Sagar Press, 1917.

Bṛhadāraṇyakopaniṣad with Śaṅkara's Commentary, AnSS 15, Poona : 1891.

Bṛhadāraṇyakopaniṣadbhāṣyavārtika with Ānandagiri's Commentary; Śāstraprakāśikā 3 vols., AnSS 16, Poona : 1892-94.

Bṛhadāraṇyakavārtikasāra of Vidyāraṇya, Chowkamba Sanskrit Series Nos. 205-208, 243-244, 257-258, 271-272, Benares: 1915-1919.

Nyāyakalpalatikā, vol. 2, (ed.) V. Subrahmanya Sastri, Tirupati : Kendriya Sanskrit Vidyapeetha, 1975.

Sambandhavārtika of Sureśvara, (ed. & tr.) T.M.P. Mahadevan, Madras : University of Madras, 1972.

BOOKS

Hino, S., *Sureśvara's Vārtika on Yājñavalkya-Maitreyī Dialogue,* Delhi : Motilal Banarsidass, 1982.

Jog, K.P. & S. Hino, *Sureśvara's Vārtika on Madhu Brāhmaṇa,* Delhi : Motilal Banarsidass, 1988.

Limaye, V.P. & R.D. Vadekar, *Eighteen Principal Upaniṣads,* vol. 1, Poona: Vaidika Samshodhana Mandala, 1958.

Madhavananda, S., (tr.) *The Bṛhadaraṇyaka Upaniṣad,* Calcutta : Advaita Ashrama, 1975.

Röer, E., (tr.) *The Twelve Principal Upaniṣads,* vol. 2, Madras : Theosophical Publishing House, 1931.

VERSE INDEX

Figure 1.1 precedes verses from BUBV 1.1.
No figure precedes verses from BUBV 1.2.